# Research Ethics & Plagiarism

# Research Ethics & Plagiarism

NASIRUDHEEN T
SREELATHA K

Ess Ess Publications
New Delhi

# Research Ethics & Plagiarism



**ISBN : 978-81-947398-7-6**

**Price : Rs. 500/-**

**First Published 2021**

Published by:
**Ess Ess Publications**
4831/24, Ansari Road,
Darya Ganj,
New Delhi-110 002.
INDIA
Phones: 23260807, 41563444
Fax: 41563334
E-mail: info@essessreference.com
www.essessreference.com

Cover Design by *Patch Creative Unit*

Printed and bound in India

# Contents

# Preface

Ethical issue in teaching, learning and research is a recent and hot issue among academic community especially after the advent of ICT revolution. In fact ethical violation has been prevailing years back. It was in the form of copying from conventional resources such as books, periodicals and theses. It was not easy to detect this misconduct. After the advent of ICT revolution, it is very easy to copy and re-use any resource. At the same time it is also easy to detect this misconduct with the help of various software packages. There is a misbelief not only among common people, but even among academic people that, internet is a free space where anything can be uploaded and anything can be downloaded. In fact there are some ethical issues in handling internet especially copyright and plagiarism issues.

Authorities have taken ethical issues in this field seriously. UGC, the biggest body of higher education in India has taken the issue of plagiarism seriously. UGC has been providing free software for plagiarism checking to all Universities in the country and declared disciplinary actions to the violation. This is book is definitely one which can give awareness regarding plagiarism. In addition to plagiarism, very important areas as far researchers are concerned have been included in the book, ie open access information resources, citation styles, research metrics and open publishing. The awareness about plagiarism is not to be confined among researchers but among whole academic community. With that optimism we submit this work to the academic world.

# Foreword

In the immediate post-independence era, academic research was mainly confined to few selected institutions which were inaccessible to common men. Even the elites in the society often preferred the reputed institutions in the west to pursue their higher education and research dreams. Hence, the rate of enrolment in for higher education was miniscule. Realizing the need for higher enrolment in higher education and research, based on the recommendations of Radahkrishnan and Kothari Commissions etc., formulated policies and took many initiatives to attract young talents to the higher education institutions of India.

The government decision to universalize higher education has paid rich dividends in the later years. The rate of enrolment graph of higher education became high. At the same time educational bodies like UGC are determined to uphold the standards, has introduced innovative measures to ensure the quality in higher education. Thus, we have reached a situation where it is practically impossible to sustain or survive in the higher education field without impactful research.

Even though teaching and research are inseparable in the higher education field, the skill set required for both are considerably different. Teaching is basically a process concerned with dissemination of already existing information, where the emphasis is on the ability to collect and communicate information in a format suitable for the recipients. But research deals with the creation or advancement of information where creativity and intellect forms the principal components which determine the effectiveness of research output. Finding the skill sets for teaching and research in the same individual is ideal but seldom found in practice. To make the matters worse, the UGC regulations for career advancement are heavily oriented towards research publications. Under these circumstances, it is noted that, there is a tendency among few individuals working in the higher education field to resort to unethical practices in the areas of research and publication to cover up their deficiency in research skills. UGC has taken serious note of it and intervened in this matter promulgating a regulation in 2018 called 'Promotion of Academic Integrity and Prevention of Plagiarism in Higher Education Institutions'. The mandatory steps required for upholding the research ethics are detailed in the regulation. In tune with the regulation, the compulsory aspects about the research ethics are included in six month course work for research scholars.

Dr. Nasirudheen T & (Dr.) Sreelatha K seasoned library and information professionals with years of experience in higher education have authored this book "**Publication ethics and plagiarism**" to provide awareness to teachers and research scholars on the topics like academic ethics, plagiarism, online information sources, open access publishing, reference management and citation styles and research metrics. I put forward this endeavour to the academic community with pleasure.

**Dr.Vinod V.M.**
*Head, Research Desk,*
*C.H.M.K. University Library,*
*University of Calicut, Kerala.*

# 1
# Academic Integrity

Integrity among academic community has been a serious issue all over the world especially after the advent of ICT revolution. Integrity means truthfulness and honesty.

## FUNDAMENTAL VALUES OF ACADEMIC DIGNITY

There are five fundamental values for academic integrity. They are :

**1. Honesty :** Academic integrity demands honesty in all academic activities such as – teaching, learning, research publication, administration etc. So it is to be practiced by teachers, students, researches, administrators, academicians etc.

**2. Trust :** Academic integrity solicits mutual trust among personnel who are engaged with academic institutions.

**3. Fairness :** Academic environment should be flourished with fair attitude in all facets and transactions. Each and every member of an institution is obliged to ensure fairness in all kinds of functions.

**4. Respect :** Respect is needed mutually among not only teacher community and student community, but also among other personnel related with academic institutions. Unfortunately it is confined between students and teachers.

Respect among all personnel constitutes the academic harmony.

**5. Responsibility:** Being responsible means taking care fulfilling the assignments allotted to each one of the academic institutions. As one subsystem fails to fulfill their duties, it will affect the whole education system.

**Center for Academic Integrity (CAI) defines academic integrity as " a commitment even a face of adversity to five fundamental values - honesty, trust, fairness, respect and responsibility "**

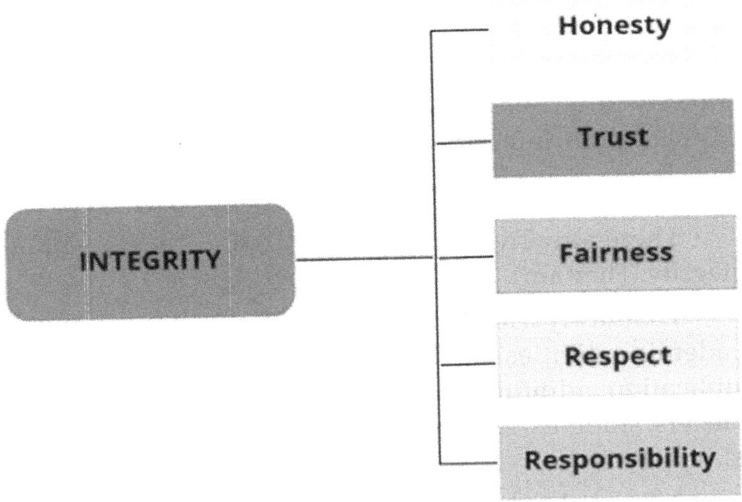


**Fig. 1. Facets of integrity**

So academic integrity means truthfulness and honesty among academic community especially in academic activities. There are mainly two types of communities in academic environment, ie **'student community'** and **'teacher community'**. Presently these two words are given explanation based on academic integrity. The following figure shows it clearly.

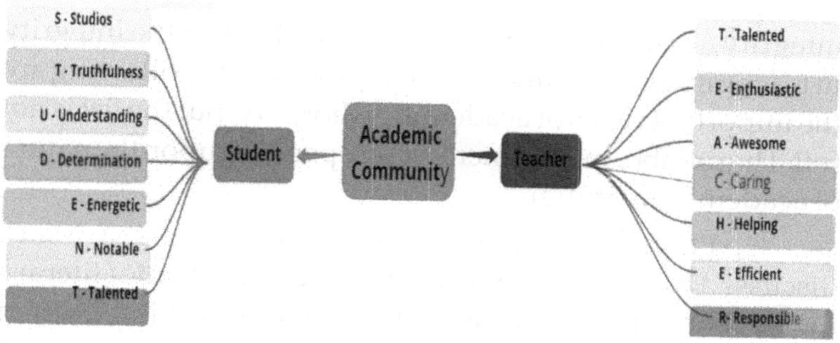


**Fig. 2. Academic community**

Academic integrity / dis-integrity has been concentrated on the following actions in the academic environment.

1. Teaching
2. Learning, and
3. Research

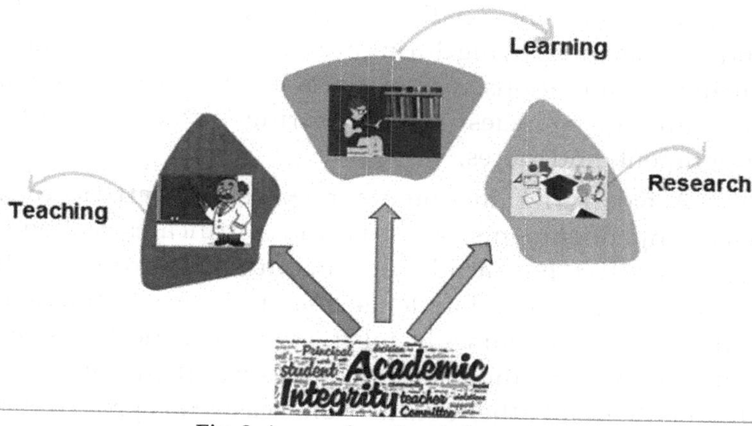


**Fig. 3. Areas of academic integrity**

Academic integrity means making use one's intellectual property, thoughts and ideas in presentations, examinations, writing books and articles etc. without further explanations (acknowledgement).

## Academic dis-integrity

It is violation of academic integrity. Academic dis-integrity/ dishonest is those deeds which affect the integrity in teaching, learning and research process. The following are the important types of academic dishonesty, but the list is not full. The number may be increased depending upon the nature of academic institution.

**1. Plagiarism :** Plagiarism is one of the hot issues discussed among academic community. Academic/ literary theft is known as plagiarism. It is a violation of intellectual property right. It can be happened intentionally and unknowingly. It means using someone else's work without giving any credit (proper citation).

**2. Cheating :** Academic cheating refers to misleading practices occurred in educational institutions. It may be personal cheating, group cheating or institutional cheating. In the academic environment cheating involves - collection and dissemination of information during examination and tests and assessment, copying during examination, impersonation during examinations, writing articles and assignments, outsourcing agencies for preparing project reports, assignments and theses.

**3. Falsifying documents, records and certificates :** Falsifying documents, records and certificates is being occurred among academic institutions from both administrative side and students' side. Students get admission and entry to new courses by falsifying the certificates. Some institutions argue they have recognition and affiliations to Universities and other boards. Some cases it is proved it is falsified.

**4. Stealing, Concealment and destruction :** These types of academic dishonesty are confined to student community. Students show their revenge to their academic institutions by practicing these types of dishonesty, such as destruction of classroom furniture, laboratory materials, computer etc., and stealing of library books, computer equipment etc.

## Reasons for academic dishonesty

**1. Academic pressure :** Academic pressure because of tight academic schedule, tight syllabus, time bounded assignments, poor standard of students etc. may lead to academic dis-integrity. During these occasions students may depend others for the fulfillment of their obligations.

**2. Desire for getting reputation :** Presently PhD degree and publications are treated as a status symbol among faculty members and reputed and high-tech courses are treated as status symbol among student community. For getting this reputation, some of them depends short cut methods which will ultimately be resulted any type of academic dis-integrity.

**3. Poor time management :** Lack of proper time management leads academic dishonesty. It is commonly seen among student community. In this case they are unaware of the preferences (what to do first and what to do later) and ultimately they depend on unfair deeds.

**4. Academic laziness :** Doing research, writing research papers, presentation of conference papers, submitting assignments and projects need dedication and hard work. Unfortunately it is lacking a few of academic members, which leads to academic dis-integrity.

**5. Lack of language proficiency :** Lack of language proficiency especially in English language will leads to violation of academic honesty.

**6. Lack of awareness of about dis-integrity :** Proper awareness about academic dis-integrity is lacking among academic community especially different types. As far as researchers are concerned it is confined to plagiarism and as far students are concerned it is confined to copying during examinations. UGC (University Grants Commission) has taken good initiative in this regard. UGC has implemented a compulsory paper for all PhD research work.

## Approaches handling academic dis-integrity

There are mainly three types of approaches in handling academic dis-integrity. They are –

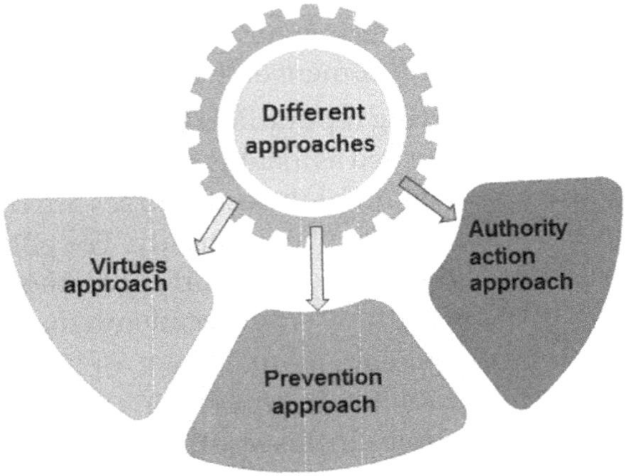


**Fig. 4. Approaches handling academic dis-integrity**

**1. Virtues approach :** This is the first and initial model to handle the academic dishonesty. It is to develop and nurture a culture of honesty among academic community.

**2. Prevention model :** According to this model, proper training in preparing research work, project reports, assignments are given through conferences, workshops, seminars/webinars etc. In addition to this awareness of after effect of academic dis-integrity is also given.

**3. Authority- action approach :** This is the last and final approach. According to this approach, the academic institutions report their higher authorities for further action and punishment. Action from the part of UGC has been announced and it will be discussed in the following chapter.

The ideal academic culture is one which is based on academic honesty. There are a lot of ingredients which mold this culture, such as attitude of organization, social and economic culture, policies of government etc. This culture has to be fostered not only in higher education level, but also from the beginning of education.

## REFERENCES

https://www.youtube.com/channel/UC8FIltjQY8pvNgz_BV0XX9Q

https://onlinecourses.swayam2.ac.in/cec20_ge37/unit?unit=36&lesson =40

https://www.slideshare.net/courosa/academic-integrity-keynote-presentation?qid=af5abbd5-4fdb-45f8-b665-ee6c0222416d &v=&b=&from_search=1

https://www.slideshare.net/thecleversheep/academic-integrity-presentation/34-Kinesthetic_Learners

www.academicintegrity.org/fundamental_values_project/index.php

https://www.stonybrook.edu/commcms/spd/assets/pdfs/dishonesty.pdf

# 2

# Publication Ethics & Plagiarism

## ETHICS IN RESEARCH

Ethics is a branch of philosophy which distinguishes between right and wrong. Ethics has been a discussion issue even from the starting of human life. An ethical issue in research is a recent and hot issue among academic community especially after the advent of ICT revolution. In fact ethical violation has been prevailing years back. It was in the form of copying from conventional resources such as books, periodicals and theses. It was not easy to detect this misconduct. After the advent of ICT revolution, it is very easy to copy and re-use any resource. At the same time it is also easy to detect this misconduct with the help of various software packages. There is a misbelief not only among common people, but even among academic people that, internet is a free space where anything can be uploaded and anything can be downloaded. In fact there are some ethical issues in handling internet especially copyright and plagiarism issues.

The following factors are considered as the facets of a good research work. Violation of any one is treated as research misconduct.

**Honesty:** Honesty has to be maintained throughout the research process (in topic selection, in literature review, data selection, data collection, data analysis, data interpretation and research reporting).

**Objectivity:** The research should not be biased. Avoid bias in research design data collection, data analysis and report writing.

**Carefulness :** Research is a careful and critical examination. So carefulness is inbuilt in research activities. Carelessness and negligence will lead wrong result and conclusion.

**Integrity :** Keep the researchers promises and agreements with sincerity; strive for consistence of thought and action.

**Communicate result :** Researchers are obliged to publish their research output before the society. The ultimate objective of the research is knowledge creation.

**Intellectual property right :** Honor copyright and other forms of IPR. Do not use unpublished data and results without permission (Refrain plagiarism).

**Confidentiality :** Protect data and communication related to research confidential. Before the data collection, a promise is given to the respondents regarding the confidentiality of information given by them and their details.

**Legality :** Get awarded and obey institutional and governmental laws.

## TYPES OF ETHICAL VIOLATIONS IN RESEARCH

- Plagiarism
- Submitting / publishing same paper to different journals
- Avoid collaborators of the paper while publishing it
- Include a person as a co-author on a paper even he did not make contribution to the paper

- Using an inappropriate statistical technique in order to enhance the significance of research
- Bypassing the peer review process
- Conducting a review of literature that fails to acknowledge the contributions

## PLAGIARISM

There are various interpretations regarding the origin of the word 'plagiarism'. The prominent among is the word 'plagiarism' was derived from the Latin word *plagiarius*, which means kidnapping. Plagiarism is using someone else's words, ideas or images as your own without proper citation. It is a dishonest, unethical, illegal, and is theft of intellectual property.

Merriam-Webster Online Dictionary (http://www.merriam-webster.com/dictionary/plagiarism.) defines, 'to plagiarize' means

- "to use the words or ideas of another person as if they were your own words or ideas"
- "to steal and pass off (the ideas or words of another) as one's own: use (another's production) without crediting the source"
- "to commit literary theft: present as new and original an idea or product derived from an existing source"

According to 'American Association of University Professors', plagiarism means, "taking over the ideas, methods, or written words of another, without acknowledgment and with the intention that they be taken as the work of the deceiver."

Rampola, defined "plagiarism is the act of taking the words, ideas, or research of another person and putting them forward without citation as if they were your own. It is intellectual theft and a clear violation of the code of ethics and behavior that most academic institutions have established to regulate the scholastic conduct of their members."

According to 'Office of Research Integrity' (ORI) plagiarism includes "both the theft or misappropriation of intellectual property and the substantial unattributed textual copying of another's work"

According to 'The University of Queensland, Australia', plagiarism is "the act of misrepresenting as one's own original work the ideas, interpretations, words or creative works of another either intentionally or unintentionally.

According to English Literary Society, plagiarism can be described as –

- "turning in someone else's work as your own;
- copying words or ideas from someone else without giving credit;
- failing to put a quotation in quotation marks;
- giving incorrect information about the source of a quotation;
- changing words but copying the sentence structure of a source without giving credit;
- copying so many words or ideas from a source that it makes up the majority of your work, whether you give credit or not".

## CATEGORIES OF PLAGIARISM

There are mainly two categories of plagiarism. They are–

**1. Intentional plagiarism :** If a person deliberately copies other material without any credit to its author in known as intentional plagiarism. It may happen both from printed and electronic sources, and copying from electronic sources are comparative easy method. Outsourcing a third party for research work / paper writing will also come under this category.

**2. Unintentional / Accidental plagiarism :**

Unintentional plagiarism happens when a person does not have any intention of plagiarism. At the same time proper references have not been given. Unintentional plagiarism also includes careless paraphrasing.

## TYPES OF PLAGIARISM

There are different types of plagiarism. Different experts have listed in different ways. Most of them have been discussed here. Even though each one deferrer in their integrity, all are considered serious academic dis-integrity.

**Fig. 5. Types of plagiarism**

**Clone type plagiarism :** Clone type plagiarism is copying full text from another source without citation and quotation. This method of plagiarism in also known as direct plagiarism and full text plagiarism. This is the highly problematic form of plagiarism.

**Self-plagiarism/auto plagiarism** : Self plagiarism is that type of plagiarism in which researcher reuse significant part of his/her previously published work without acknowledgment. This type of plagiarism is mostly seen among research scholars and faculty. The solution of this type is self-citation (citing one's own works). Self- plagiarism will also occur as one author takes full works or a portion of his previous work having authors other than him without others consent and citation. This is also called as recycle plagiarism.

**Cntrl+C plagiarism :** It is the copying of significant portion of a paper and pastes it for forming a new paper without citation.

**Find & replace method of plagiarism :** As per this method of plagiarism, keywords in a source paper are identified and are replaced with synonyms of the keywords without losing the essential content.

**Re-mix type of plagiarism :** It is the copying and paraphrasing sentences from different sources and forming a single paper. This is also known as Mosaic plagiarism and patch work plagiarism.

**Hybrid form of plagiarism :** It is the combination of perfectly cited source and copied source without proper citation.

**Aggregator type plagiarism :** If a scholar gives correct citation and the paper contains no original work. There is no relation with paper and citation.

**Source based plagiarism/404 error type :** source based plagiarism is that type of plagiarism, where a researcher gives incorrect citation which does not exist. Using the secondary data and giving the primary source's citation also comes under source based plagiarism.

**Inaccurate authorship :** inaccurate authorship plagiarism will be occurred in two ways. The first way is, when an individual prepares a manuscript but he/she does not get the credit for it (his/her name is not mentioned anywhere). The second form the other side of this coin, ie. when an individual gets credit without any action. This is equal to copy the full manuscript and change the author's name.

## DIFFERENT WAYS OF AVOIDING PLAGIARISM (Nagpal, Bharti 2018)

**Citation :** giving proper citation is the main weapon to avoid plagiarism. There are different types of citation styles like APA, MLA, Chicago etc. Normally the institution/ journals will insist the type of citation style for research report and journal article. If there is no instruction, any standard type can be taken, but consistency of citation style has to be maintained throughout the work.

**Quoting :** if one writes the words of an author as it is from an original source, then it is to be written with in the double quotation. The words in the double quotation should not be exceeded more than 40. It is not good to use more quotations in a single paper, but better to use paraphrasing.

**Paraphrasing :** after reading the original work and rephrasing one's own words is known as paraphrasing. It is better not to write more than three words in continuation as given in the original work.

**Citing own work :** Using own previously done work without citation comes under the type of plagiarism. It can be avoided by giving self-citation.

**Referencing :** At the end of research report and journal articles (academic writing) bibliographic details of each source from where ideas, information, data etc. have been taken. It is also written as per the rules of citation style.

**Become honest :** Honesty is the quality to be maintained not only in research but throughout in life.

## CAUSES OF PLAGIARISM (Kiran Rani 2018)

**1. Lack of language proficiency :** conventional system of education ( radio type) lacks creativity, skills of expression etc. But recently the system of education has been changed and its result can be expected among new generation. The skill of writing needs special attention in the form of input-rich environment along with providing opportunities for output. In the absence of this, there will be a tendency of copying from other sources, beginning from friends' note books and ending in sources from internet.

**2. Lack of subject proficiency :** Students who do not have subject proficiency are forced to plagiarize in order to complete their assignments/ project works. In order to avoid this, from the very beginning of the courses keen attention is need. Then only students can complete their thesis/ dissertation at the end of the course.

**3. Topic being generic** : If the research topic or assignment question is too generic, a lot of resources are available in printed and electronic form. Students may feel easy to complete their works by copying and pasting from sources from internet.

**4. Ignorance of citation and style manuals :** Lack of knowledge of citation and different citation styles among students lead unintentional plagiarism. One way to avoid committing this type of plagiarism is to install any reference management software such as mendeley, reference manager etc. Reference management is also available in online. Output gets as bibliographic details enters in to the software and select the style manual.

**5. Lack of clarity about "common knowledge" :** Common knowledge is exempted from citation. Examples of common language are – 'sun risers from east', 'earth moves around the sun'. It is however different with 'commonly available sources that need citation'. Sources like dictionary, encyclopedia, newspaper etc. will require citations; by failing it will leads to plagiarism.

**6. Lack of plagiarism policy :** Plagiarism policy is the legal protection of plagiarism. In India, UGC has implemented plagiarism policy recently. But in the colleges, this is not properly checked. Proper awareness of plagiarism policy is to be given to the students.

**7. Dis-interest in course :** if a student does not have interest in course, students depends short cut methods such as plagiarism in order to complete their assignments and projects.

**8. Loss of faith in good values :** If a person does not believe on academic well-being / honesty, he will do anything as he wishes.

## PLAGIARISM DETECTION

Plagiarism detection can be executed in two ways, manual checking and machine (software) checking. The former one is the traditional procedure which is a time consuming process and its scope is limited to print resources. The latter is software based plagiarism checking and it used widely. There are different types of plagiarism checking software which give output as not plagiarism, but similarity with other available online resources.

Different commercial and free plagiarism detection software packages are available now. The prominent among are –

- iThenticate
- Turnitin
- Writecheck
- Plagiarism.org
- Plagtracker.com
- Writecheck
- Duplichecker
- Plagscanner
- Plagetracker
- Viper, etc.

Content coverage is the main feature of this type of software. It is recommended to use software with high content coverage. There are certain limitations to the software.

No software is 100% perfect in this regard. Some of the limitations are :

- Regional / vernacular languages are not supported by most of the software.
- Year blindness (software do not recognize which one is recently published and which one is old one.)
- Do not recognize mathematical formulae.
- Problems with identification of tables, graphs and images.

## HUMAN INTERVENTION

Software packages are giving out put as similarity with other available online resources. Similarity does not mean plagiarism. After getting the similarity result, a manual checking is needed for final verdict. Common knowledge is exempted from the similarity result. In addition to common knowledge, special vocabularies, usage, formulae etc. in a specific field is also to be exempted.

The following are some of the examples of common knowledge.

- Listing of important personalities
- Significant historical event dates
- Terms in use over a period of time
- Text known to a particular community, which need not be credited within the community that is familiar with, but it, is to be credited outside the community.

## PENALTIES OF PLAGIARISM

If a person is found guilty, the following will be legal action.

- Requirement for submission of new or alternative piece of work.
- Withdrawing of research scholarships.

- Total or partial loss of marks in the examinations or assignment or course in which the misconduct is occurred.
- Suspension or expulsion from college/University.
- Recommendation for revocation/rescinding of degree.

If an academician is found guilty, the penalties will be –

- Legal action from the state.
- Humiliation to the credibility of both individual and institution.
- Disciplinary action as per the institutional law
- Suspension or expulsion from job.
- Blocking of increments and other benefits
- Debarment from eligibility to receive research funds for grants and contract from any government agency.

## PENALTIES INSISTED BY UGC (UNIVERSITY GRANTS COMMISSION – NEW DELHI)

UGC has categorized plagiarism as 4 levels based on the similarity with other source. They are –

- Level 0 – similarities up to 10 %
- Level 1 – similarities above 10 % to 40%
- Level 2 - similarities above 40 % to 60%
- Level 3 - similarities above 60 %

### Penalties of plagiarism in the case of thesis and dissertation

**Level 0 :** Similarities up to 10% - Minor Similarities, no penalty.

**Level 1 :** Similarities above 10% to 40% - Such student shall be asked to submit a revised script within a stipulated time period not exceeding 6 months.

**Level 2 :** Similarities above 40% to 60% - Such student

shall be debarred from submitting a revised script for a period of one year.

**Level 3 :** Similarities above 60% -Such student registration for that programme shall be cancelled.

In the case of repetition, such students shall be punished one level higher than the previous level committed by him/ her. If plagiarism is proved after the date of award of degree or credit as the case may be then his/her degree or credit shall be put in pending for a period recommended by the Institutional Academic Integrity Panel and by the Head of the Institution.

## Penalties in the case of plagiarism in academic and research publications.

**Level 0 :** Similarities up to 10% - Minor similarities, no penalty.

**Level 1 :** Similarities above 10% to 40%

(a) Shall be asked to withdraw manuscript

**Level 2 :** Similarities above 40% to 60%

(a) Shall be asked to withdraw manuscript.

(b) Shall be denied a right to one annual increment.

(c) Shall not be allowed to be a supervisor to any new Master's, M.Phil., Ph.D. Student/scholar for a period of two years.

**Level 3 :** Similarities above 60%

(a) Shall be asked to withdraw manuscript.

(b) Shall be denied a right to two successive annual increments.

(c) Shall not be allowed to be a supervisor to any new Master's, M.Phil., Ph.D. Student/scholar for a period of three years.

## PLAGIARISM & COPYRIGHT INFRINGEMENT

Plagiarism is using someone else' work or ideas without

giving proper credit. It is unethical and academic dishonesty, while copyright infringement It is using others' work without permission or compensation. It is a legal offence. The difference between plagiarism and copyright infringement is given below (Ohio State University libraries, nd)

| | Plagiarism | Copyright infringment |
|---|---|---|
| **What is it?** | **Occurs when one person use someone else' words or ideas without giving credit** | It occurs when you violate exclusive rights of an author/creator (reproduce or make copies, display in public, perform the work publicly etc.) |
| **Governing rules** | Academic institutions follows codes/rules for plagiarism | Copyright laws of each countries governs copyrights of authors/ producers of that country |
| **Offence against** | Author | Copyright holder |
| **How to avoid** | Credit the source always and when summarise or paraphrase materials, restate it in your own words. | .Determine if your use falls under a statutory exception, such as Fair Use<br>• Comply with existing license terms or terms of use if available<br>• Request permission from the copyright owner to use the work |
| **Enforcing Agency** | Instructors, research guides and institutions as a whole may enforce penalties for plagiarism | A copyright owner or his authorized agent may bring a claim of copyright infringement. It may be settled in or out court |

## CONCLUSION

Plagiarism is discussed in PG level and PhD level. But the process of plagiarism is starting from the school level. By getting the assignment questions, students "Google" the question or keyword and copy paste the answer from the internet without giving any reference. Even in the case of PhD level, plagiarism is discussed only in the time of research reporting. It has to be started along with the initial step of research process. So a strong awareness on plagiarism is to be done among academic community by various programmes such as – seminars, workshops, conferences etc. The new step of UGC to include a paper entitled "Research & publication ethics" for researchers all over India is appreciable. It is an ideal step to Universities in international level.

## REFERENCES

American Association of University Professors (September/October, 1989). "Statement on Plagiarism." *Academe, 75*, 5, 47-48.

Kiran Rani (2018). Academic writing and issues pertaining to plagiarism. In. In Vinod kumar Kanvaria, Academic writing, anti-plagiarism and citations. Shipra publications, Delhi, pp 104-118.

Merriam-Webster Online Dictionary, *http://www.merriam-*

Rampolla, Mary Lynn, *A Pocket Guide to Writing History*, 4th edition, New York: Boston, 2004, 70-76, https://www.coursehero.com/file/27286454/avoiding-plagerismpdf/.ORI Policy on Plagiarism" https://ori.hhs.gov/ori-policy- plagiarism.

University of Queensland, Library, Australia,

https://www.uq.edu.au/search/?q=%20&as_sitesearch=library.uq.edu.au

*http://www.eliterarysociety.com/what-is-plagiarism/*

Nagpal, Bharti (2018). Plagiarism- a major concern in academic writing. In Vinod Kanvaria in Academic writing, anti-plagiarism and citations. Shipra publication, Delhi.p 47-59

webster.com/dictionary/plagiarism

# 3

# Electronic Information Resources/E-resources

Dictionary of Library and Information Science defines e-resources as "material consisting of data and/ or computer program(s) encoded for reading and manipulation by a computer by the use of a peripheral device directly connected to the computer or remotely via a network such as the Internet. The category includes software application, electronic text, bibliographic databases, etc" (Reitz, 2005).

Any information that is accessible through computer, network, e-book reader, notebook, mobile phone or any other handheld device can be termed as digital information, electronic information and ICT based information resources. After the advent of ICT the conventional form of information resources has been changed as e-resources, such as books became e-books, journals became e-journal; thesis became e-thesis and so on. As the e-resources are available freely, which are termed as open access resources.

## ADVANTAGES OF E-RESOURCES

There are a number of unique features and advantages for e-resources over printed resources. (Chandal, A.S & MukeshSaikia, 2012). They are:-

**1. Multi users accessibility :** In this case 'n' number of users can access the same resources by using multiple access points such as computers, laptops, e-book readers or even smart phones. Problem of multiplicity of the resources is unimportant in the case of e-resources.

**2. Speed :** Speed is the unique feature of ICT revolution. The problem of delay has been vanished. Publishing, circulation, copying, downloading and printing are very speedy.

**3. Round the clock availability :** Round the clock accessibility is another unique feature of e-resources. It can be possible 24X7 days and 365 days irrespective of working hours and working days.

**4. No physical boundary :** E-resources can be accessed anywhere in the world on the condition of availability of Internet connectivity. Users would need not to physically visit the libraries.

**5. Searching is very easy :** Users can search through multiple point of view. It is possible on – author, title, subject, publisher and keywords.

**6. Integration of multi-formats :** E-resources would support texts, images, graphics and audio & video formats.

**7. Less storage space :** Less storage space is enough to store e-resources. Thousands of resources can be stored in a small chip.

**8. Book marking facility :** It is possible to bookmark the favorite resources of users.

**9. Preservation and Archiving :** Preservation without harm and archiving for future use is very easy in the case of e-resources.

**10. Networking :** A particular electronic resource or source of resource can be networked with others. So resource sharing is very easy.

**11. Cost-effective :** Printing, binding and postage charges can be eliminated. No need of much storage space like buildings and shelves. So it is economical.

**12.** Can be downloaded instantly.

**13.** Physical dis-abled users can access with the help of assistive technologies.

**14.** Do not require bindery and repair.

**15.** Do not needed shelving and rectification.

## PROMINENT ONLINE E-RESOURCES

Prominent e-resources open access ad paid, both national level and international level have been briefly described below. Most of them are initiatives of government of India.

### 1. National digital library of India (https://ndl.iitkgp.ac.in) - Open source

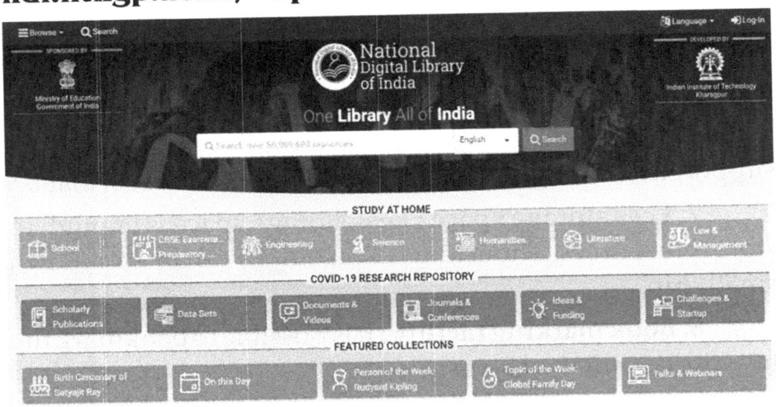


**Fig. 6. Home page of NDLI**

National digital library of India was started in 2006. It is an initiative of Ministry of Human Resource & Development (MHRD), government of India (presently Department of Education). It is developed, operated and maintained by IIT (Indian Institute of Technology) Kharagpur. It is designed to hold content of any language and provide interface support for

10 Indian languages. Registration and login is needed for accessing this resource. This is an open access e-resource.

**Features**

- All types of resources such as - books, audios, videos, presentations, question papers etc. are available.
- Educational materials from primary to post graduate level are available.
- Subject coverage - technology, social science, literature, law, medicine etc.
- Different searching facilities are available.
  - by type ( audio, video, image, text, presentation, animation).
  - by subject ( three levels as listed in DDC, ie in first level there are 10 basic subjects, in second level 100 subjects and in third level 1000 subjects.
  - by source ( NCERT, GATE, world e-book library, shodhganga).
  - by resource type (article, book, question papers, thesis etc.)

## 2. SWAYAM (Study Web of Active learning for Young Aspiring Minds). (https://swayam.gov.in)

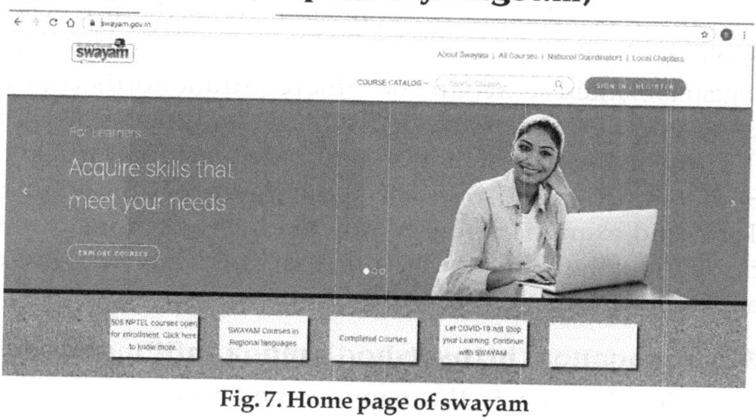


**Fig. 7. Home page of swayam**

It is the national platform of MOOC (massive open online course) government of India. It is an initiative of Ministry of Human Resource & Development (MHRD), (presently Department of Education). There are hundreds of courses with duration of 4 weeks to 24 weeks.

SWAYAM is the umbrella of MOOC courses of 9 national co-coordinators. They are -

- AICTE (All India Council of Technical Education)
- CEC (Consortium for Education Communication)
- IGNOU (Indira Gandhi National Open University)
- IIM (Indian Institute of Management) Bangalore
- NCERT (National Council for Educational Research & Training)
- NIOS (National Institute of Open Schooling)
- NITTR (National Institute of Technical Teachers Training & Research)
- NPTEL (National Programme on Technology Enhanced Learning)
- UGC (University Grants Commission)

MOOC courses are free, which need no education qualification and age restriction. SWAYAM app is available and which is available in playstore. Users are needed to register and enter by using user name and password. Students can register for interested course once the registration of the course is started. The registered students will get study materials (pdf documents, ppt presentation and video lectures) weekly. Students are needed to submit the assignment time to time. Term end examination is conducted in selected institutes throughout the country. The course is completely free where as certain fee is levied for getting the certificate.

### 3. Shodhganga (https://shodhganga.inflibnet.ac.in)

Shodhganga is the name coined to denote digital

repository of Indian electronic theses and dissertation set up by INFLIBNET Centre. The word "shodh" originates from Sanskrit and stands for research and discovery. The "Ganga" is the holiest, largest and longest of all rivers in Indian subcontinent. The Ganga is the symbol of India's age-long culture and civilization, ever-changing, ever-flowing, ever-loved and revered by its people, and has held India's heart captive and dawn uncounted millions to her banks since the dawn of history.

Presently there are more than 2,90,000 electronic theses. Presently 561 Indian Universities have signed MOU with Inflibnet and 460 Universities have started uploading e-theses. Elaborated searching facility has been made available in the repository.

Searching can be done –

- by University
- by subject
- by title
- by research supervisor
- by research scholar and
- by keyword

The Shodhganga is set-up using an open source digital repository software called DSpace.

## 4. Shodhgangotri (https://shodhgangotri.inflibnet.ac.in)

Shodhgangotri is the reservoir of Indian research in progress (synopsis). He word **"Shodh"** originates from Sanskrit and stands for "research and discovery". **"Gangotri"** is one of the largest glaciers in the Himalayas and source of origination of Ganges, the holiest, longest and largest of rivers in India. Under the initiative called **"ShodhGangotri"**, research scholars / research supervisors in universities are requested to deposit electronic version of approved synopsis submitted by research scholars to the universities for registering themselves for the Ph.D programme Now it is expanded to MRPs/PDFs/ Emeritus Fellowship etc.

Searching can be done –

- by University
- by subject
- by title
- by research supervisor
- by research scholar and
- by keyword

The repository on one hand, would reveal the trends and directions of research being conducted in Indian universities, on the other hand it would avoid duplication of research.

## 5. E-shodhsindhu

E-ShodhSindhu was formed by merging three consortia initiatives, namely UGC-INFONET Digital Library Consortium, NLIST and INDEST-AICTE Consortium. The e-ShodhSindhu will continue to provide current as well as archival access to more than 10,000 core and peer-reviewed journals and a number of bibliographic, citation and factual databases in different disciplines from a large number of publishers and aggregators to its member institutions including centrally-funded technical institutions, universities and colleges. The main objective of the e-ShodhSindu: Consortia for Higher Education E-Resources is to provide access to qualitative electronic resources including full-text, bibliographic and factual databases to academic institutions at a lower rates of subscription.

## 6. Swayam Prabha (https://www.swayamprabha.gov.in/index.php/home)

The SWAYAM PRABHA is a group of 34 DTH channels devoted to telecasting of high-quality educational programmes on 24X7 basis using the GSAT-15 satellite. Every day, there will be new content for at least (4) hours which would be repeated 5 more times in a day, allowing the students to choose the time of their convenience. The channels are uplinked from BISAG, Gandhinagar. The contents are provided by NPTEL, IITs, UGC, CEC, IGNOU, NCERT and NIOS. The INFLIBNET Centre maintains the web portal.

Coverage of DTH channels –

- Higher education – curriculum based course contents at post graduate and under graduate level covering diverse discipline
- School level education (9th - 12th class).
- Curriculum based course that can meet the needs of lifelong learners.
- Assist students ( 11th &12th ) prepare for competitive examinations.

The main motive of swayam prabha is to provide access e-resources especially in the remote areas of India where internet connectivity is poor.

### 7. Directory of Open access Journals (DOAJ) –( https://doaj.org)

The DOAJ (Directory of Open Access Journals) was launched in 2003 with 300 open access journals. Today, this independent database contains over 15 000 peer-reviewed open access journals and 48 lakh articles covering all areas of science, technology, medicine, social sciences, arts and humanities. Presently the collection covers 80 languages from 123 countries.

### 8. Directory of open Access Books (DOAB) – https://www.doabooks.org

DOAB is a searchable database of metadata of free share e-books by different publishers throughout the world. The primary aim of DOAB is to increase discoverability of Open

Access books. Academic publishers are invited to provide metadata of their Open Access books to DOAB. Metadata will be harvestable in order to maximize dissemination, visibility and impact. The directory is open to all publishers who publish academic, peer reviewed books in Open Access and should contain as many books as possible, provided that these publications are in Open Access and meet academic standards.

### 9. Networked Digital Library of Theses and Dissertations (NDLTD) - http://www.ndltd.org

The Networked Digital Library of Theses and Dissertations (NDLTD) is an international organization dedicated to promoting the adoption, creation, use, dissemination, and preservation of electronic theses and dissertations (ETDs). It supports electronic publishing and open access to scholarship in order to enhance the sharing of knowledge worldwide.

The National Digital Library of Theses and Dissertations was established in 1996, directed by an informal steering committee. As its scope became international, the organization kept the acronym NDLTD, but changed its name to the Networked Digital Library of Theses and Dissertations. Today, the NDLTD's members include hundreds of universities around the world, as well as partner organizations, including: Adobe, the American Library Association, the Association of Research Libraries, the Coalition for Networked Information, the Joint Information Services Committee, OCLC Online Computer Library Center, Proquest/UMI, and Theses Canada – all working toward the goal of unlocking the benefits of shared knowledge for all.

### 10. National Repository of Open Educational Resources (NROER) http://www.nroer.in

National Repository of Open Educational Resources is initiated by the Department of School Education and Literacy, Ministry of Human Resource Development, Government of

India and the Central Institute of Educational Technology, National Council of Educational Research and Training, The Repository belongs to all of us. Anyone can participate in, contribute, curate and organize resources and activities, growing it to reach every teacher and every student in all languages.

NROER resource library is organized in videos, audios, interactives, images and documents sections. Video Collection is organized subject wise and given short duration videos. Audio Collection is basically a collection of audio story of famous scientists, social workers, renowned personalities and other. Interactive library is a collection of simulations on various topics. The simulations are from mathematics, chemistry and physics.

## 11. eGyankosh - http://egyankosh.ac.in

eGyankosh is national digital repository to store, index, preserve, distribute and share the digital learning resources developed by the Open and distance learning institutions in the country. eGyankosh is created and maintained by IGNOU. There are five communities in this repository. They are - IGNOU FB live record videos, IGNOU self-learning materials (LMS), IGNOU SWAYAM course contents, IGNOU YouTube videos and Indian journal of open learning (IJOL).

## 12. e-PG pathsala http://epgp.inflibnet.ac.in

e-PG pathsala is an initiative of MHRD, Government of India under its national mission on education through ICT being executed by UGC. It is a system having high quality, curriculum based e-contents in 70 subjects across all disciplines of social science, humanities, arts, fine arts, natural and mathematical science.

## 13. Vidya-mitra http://vidyamitra.inflibnet.ac.in

Vidya-mitra is an online learning portal for all the e-content projects developed under the NME-ICT (National

Mission on Education through Information and Communication Technology), MHRD. The portal provides facility to search and browse all hosted content wherein a learner can easily access the desired material including audio/ video learning material, textual material, multimedia-enriched materials etc. through a single interface. Moreover, features of faceted search, usage statistics, project-wise access, My-Space are incorporated in this portal.

### 14. National Programme on Technology Enhanced Learning (NPTEL) https://nptel.ac.in/

The National Programme on Technology Enhanced Learning (NPTEL) was initiated by seven Indian Institutes of Technology (Bombay, Delhi, Kanpur, Kharagpur, Madras, Guwahati and Roorkee) along with the Indian Institute of Science, Bangalore in 2003. Five core disciplines were identified, namely, civil engineering, computer science and engineering, electrical engineering, electronics and communication engineering and mechanical engineering and 235 courses in web/ video format were developed in this phase.

### 15. The World Bank Open Knowledge Repository (OKR) https://openknowledge.worldbank.org

The World Bank Open Knowledge Repository (OKR) is The World Bank's official open access repository for its research outputs and knowledge products. Through the OKR, The World Bank collects, disseminates, and permanently preserves its intellectual output in digital form. The OKR also increases the range of people who can discover and access Bank content – from governments and civil society organizations (CSOs), to students and the general public. Since its launch in 2012, millions of publications have been downloaded from the OKR, and nearly half of its users are in developing countries.

## CONCLUSION

'Open access' is a revolution in the information dissemination. Government of India has taken good initiatives in the open access information revolution. Most of them have been describe above. Presently it is prestige issue among publishing industry to give free access to their information resource. That is why; commercial publishers are also giving some of their collection as open access. Some of the examples are – Springer open journals, Taylor & Franis open access, IEEE open access etc.

## REFERENCES


- https://ndl.iitkgp.ac.in
- https://swayam.gov.in
- https://shodhganga.inflibnet.ac.in
- https://shodhgangotri.inflibnet.ac.in
- https://www.swayamprabha.gov.in/index.php/home
- https://doaj.org
- https://www.doabooks.org
- http://www.ndltd.org
- http://www.nroer.in
- http://egyankosh.ac.in
- http://epgp.inflibnet.ac.in
- http://vidyamitra.inflibnet.ac.in
- https://openknowledge.worldbank.org

# 4

# Referencing Mechanism and Citation Tools for Academic Writing

Academic writing is generally a process of bringing out one's idea or thought as a document. It may be an article, a book chapter, a book, a blog, or any other content. To elaborate on the idea and authoritatively explain the topic, the findings, or results of a study the author has to thoroughly go through the literature and develop a background on the subject. To express what he has learned or understood and to relate this to his work, the author has to use the content or the idea of others, their style, methodology, etc., In such cases, proper credit has to be given to those authors or contributors. Failing to do so will call for plagiarism and breach of academic integrity. Fair use of works by others is allowed on providing proper citations and acknowledging the works by others. References give more credibility to the document and the reader can trace more records that are relevant to the topic.

## CITATIONS, REFERENCES, AND BIBLIOGRAPHIES

Citations and references are complimentary terms in the case of academic writing. Citations are in-text citations that direct to source references made at the end of the work. References or work cited list should cover all the citations given within the text. The work cited has a direct impact on one's work. The bibliography is a list of all the sources that the author has consulted for completing his/her work.

While going through an article or a book we may come across different citations within the text. These are given as per the style manuals.

The bibliography covers whatever sources you have consulted for the research work, it may contain the sources which you have not cited. The bibliography is arranged alphabetically and the format has to comply with style guides that you follow.

## STYLE MANUALS

Style manuals are a guide to writing and designing documents. A set of rules and standards are set forth in these manuals. Thousands of style guides are there for use. It depends on the author to adopt which style manual for doing his work and the purpose of writing the document. The style guides are set for a particular discipline, organization, or publisher/publication. The style guides help us to stick to a standard writing format like formatting, citations, and bibliographies.

Style manuals dictate the rules on preparing a paper, it's form, shape, paragraphing, punctuations, numbering, etc., and some manuals tell us how to approach the subject matter of your paper. It also describes how to put tables and graphs and pictures and their numbering styles. The most important about style guides are they put forth a standard format to give citations, references, and bibliographies. The manuals are consulted at the final stage of research for writing the research paper. The most used Style Guides are the APA Manual, MLA Style Manual, Chicago Manual, IEEE Style, Harvard Style, AMA Style, and many others. Many organizations have their own style manuals of internal and external publications.

## PUBLICATION MANUAL OF THE AMERICAN PSYCHOLOGICAL ASSOCIATION (APA) (https://library.westernsydney.edu.au/main/sites/default/files/pdf/cite_APA.pdf)

Generally called the APA Style Manual is intended for behavioral and social sciences. The latest edition (7th edition) was published in 2019. This edition was updated with guidelines for reducing bias in the language in 2020. APA style manual is widely used by scholars because of its simplicity. The new version is accessible, which means it can be read with screen readers. APA style guide helps scholarly communication and enables authors to present their work in an organised manner. The consistency of the work helps readers to focus on the ideas given by the author. The style manual serves as a torch bearer to the writing process. The APA style manual deals with scholarly writing, publishing, paper elements and formatting journal articles, reporting standards, style, grammar, language usage, tables and figures, paragraphing, numbering , headings, work cited in text and reference lists.

As per the APA style manual, an author uses the author-date citation style within the text and the details in the reference list. Some examples are here : Referencing consists of two parts, **In-text citation and references.**

## BOOKS AND CHAPTERS

SINGLE AUTHOR

| Reference list | Copstead, L., & Banasik, J. (2005). *Pathophysiology* (3rd ed.). Saunders. |
|---|---|
| In-text citation | Copstead and Banasik<br>(2005) stated that . . . or<br>It is suggested that. . . (Copstead & Banasik, 2005). |

## TWO AUTHORS

| | |
|---|---|
| Reference list | Andreasen, N. C. (2001). *Brave new brain: Conquering mental illness in the era of the genome*. Oxford University Press. |
| In-text citation | Andreasen<br>(2001)<br>stated that...<br>or<br>It is suggested that... (Andreasen, 2001). |

## THREE TO TWENTY AUTHORS

| | |
|---|---|
| Reference list | Schneider, Z., Whitehead, D., & Elliott, D. (2007). *Nursing and midwifery research: Methods and appraisal for evidence-based practice* (3rd ed.). Elsevier Australia.<br>*Note: Within each entry, author names should be listed in the order in which they appear on the source or as displayed on the title page.* |
| In-text citation | *Note: Give the name of the first author and abbreviate the others to* et al. *("and others").*<br>Schneider et al.<br>(2007) showed that<br>... or<br>... is demonstrated (Schneider et al., 2007). |

## TWENTY ONE OR MORE AUTHORS

| | |
|---|---|
| Reference list | *All authors should be given when there are up to 20 authors. If a source has 21 or more authors, place three ellipsis points between the 19th and final author name to indicate that some names have been omitted e.g.* Jones, P., . . . Adams, N. (2009).<br>Quliyev, T., Gjoni, H., Gruber, I., Hofer, S., Fischer, I., Maes, S., López, N., Díaz, O.,<br>Cruz, T., Mora, A., Wáng, R., Li, E., Yáng, A., Zhào, L., Zhôu, B., Mirza, O., Bonik, O., Aliyev, K., Biton, H., . . . Ishii, F. (2020). *Referencing styles that changed the world.* Libtty Press. |
| In-text citation | *Note: Give the name of the first author and abbreviate the others to* et al. *("and others").*<br>Quliyev et al.<br>(2020)<br>found . . .<br>or<br>This has indicated . . . (Quliyev et al., 2020). |

| | |
|---|---|
| Reference list | Narungga Aboriginal Progress Association. (2006). *Nharrangga warra: Narungga dictionary.*<br>*Note: When the author is also the publishing body omit the publisher element after the title.* |
| In-text citation | *A group author with a long name can be abbreviated in text, if it is well known or will be cited more than three times. Use the full name on the first occasion followed by the abbreviation.*<br>First entry:<br>Narungga Aboriginal Progress Association (NAPA, 2006) documents. . . or<br>Information is . . . (Narungga Aboriginal Progress Association [NAPA], 2006).<br>Second and subsequent entries: NAPA (2006) shows that . . .<br>or<br>A dictionary that . . . (NAPA, 2006) |

## GROUP AUTHOR

## NO AUTHOR

| | |
|---|---|
| Reference list | *When a work has no identifiable author, move the title of the work to the author position and follow with the date of publication.*<br>*HIV/AIDs resources: A nationwide directory* (10th ed.). (2004). Guides for Living.<br>Only use "Anonymous" in the author position if "Anonymous" is specifically stated as the author on the publication itself.<br>Anonymous. (2002). *Maximum security: A hacker's guide to protecting your computer systems and network* (4th ed.). Sams Publishing. |
| In-text citation | *When citing or referring to a title in text, capitalise all major words. If the title is long, it can be shortened for the in-text citation.*<br>*HIV/AIDs Resources*<br>(2004) states that . . . or<br>This directory shows . . . (*HIV/AIDs Resources*, 2004). Computer and network security . . . (Anonymous, 2002).<br>*Note: When giving a title in the text, capitalise all major words. If the title is long, it can be shortened for the in-text citation.* |

## EDITED BOOK

| | |
|---|---|
| Reference list | Craven, I. (Ed.). (2001). *Australian cinema in the 1990s.* Frank Cass.<br>*Note : When there is more than one editor, add (Eds.) in brackets after the last editor's name and follow the same formatting shown in the examples for books.* |
| In-text citation | Craven (2001) discussed<br>the successful . . . or<br>The film starred actors . . . (Craven, 2001). |

## CHAPTER, ARTICLE OR SECTION IN A BOOK

| | |
|---|---|
| Reference list | *For a section in an authored book, provide a reference entry for the whole book and add the chapter, article or section page numbers in the in-text citation.*<br>Knowles, M. S. (1986). *Using learning contracts.* Jossey-Bass. |
| In-text citation | Knowles (1986, pp. 73-90) demonstrated that . . . or<br>This independent study showed . . . (Knowles, 1986, pp. 12-16 ). |

## CHAPTER OR ARTICLE IN AN EDITED BOOK

| | |
|---|---|
| Reference list | Ferres, K. (2001). Idiot box: Television, urban myths and ethical scenarios. In I.<br>Craven (Ed.), *Australian cinema in the 1990s* (pp. 175-188). Frank Cass. |
| In-text citation | Ferres (2001) discussed the television episode . . . or<br>The television episode . . . (Ferres, 2001). |

## E-BOOK AVAILABLE VIA LIBRARY DATABASE

| | |
|---|---|
| Reference list | *Most library databases are academic research databases which means that the same book may be available across different databases. Therefore, APA 7 does not require database information in an e-book reference. Examples of academic research databases for ebooks are: Ebook Central, ClinicalKey, EBSCO ebooks Collection, ProQuest Central or Books@Ovid.*<br>When a DOI is available add it to the end of the reference as a URL. Start the URL with https://doi.org/<br>Hirotsu, H. (2017). *Advanced analysis of variance.* John Wiley & Sons. https://doi.org/10.1002/9781119303374<br>When there is no DOI, cite the book in the same format as a printed work.<br>Storey, K. B. (2004). *Functional metabolism: Regulation and adaptation.* John Wiley & Sons. |
| In-text citation | Storey (2004) stated that . . . or<br>Functional metabolism is . . . (Storey, 2004). |

## E-BOOK AVAILABLE VIA THE INTERNET (E.G. KINDLE BOOK) WITH NO DOI

| Reference list | Barley, E. (2016). *Health psychology in nursing practice.* SAGE Publications. https://amzn.to/2QBXtxF<br>Note: In this example the publisher name is in capital letters because it follows the same format that is displayed on the work and the URL has been shortened. |
|---|---|
| In-text citation | Barley (2016) stated that... or<br>Functional metabolism is ... (Barley, 2016). |

## JOURNAL ARTICLES, NEWSPAPER ARTICLES AND CONFERENCE PAPERS

The format for more than one author is the same for all sources including journal articles, therefore, refer to the examples for books in this guide.

## JOURNAL ARTICLE (PRINT VERSION)

| Reference list | Woolley, T., & Raasch, B. (2005). Predictors of sunburn in north Queensland recreational boat users. *Health Promotion Journal of Australia, 16*(1), 26-31.<br>*Note: If a DOI is available for a printed article include it at the end of the reference as a URL e.g.* https://doi.org/10.1177/1049732312468251 |
|---|---|
| In-text citation | Woolley and Raasch (2005)<br>stated that the ... or<br>Sunscreen is the most popular form of sun protection (Woolley & Raasch, 2005). |

# JOURNAL ARTICLE (FROM LIBRARY DATABASE)

| Reference list | *Most library databases are academic research databases. Works from these types of databases are usually available across multiple platforms, so a database name or database URL is considered irrelevant as location information in a reference.*<br>Examples of academic research databases are: Proquest, EBSCOhost, CINAHL, JSTOR, MEDLINE, Ebook Central, Science Direct, Scopus or Academic Search Complete.<br>*When a DOI is available add it to the end of the reference as a URL. Start the URL with* https://doi.org/<br>van Heugten, K. (2013). Resilience as an underexplored outcome of workplace bullying. *Qualitative Health Research, 23*(3), 291-301. https://doi.org/10.1177/1049732312468251<br>When there is no DOI, cite the work in the same manner as a journal article in a printed format.<br>Butler, K., & Gardiner, R. (2019). Daylesford longhouse: Partners Hill. *Architecture Australia, 108*(4), 68-74. |
|---|---|
| In-text citation | Butler and Gardiner (2019)<br>state that . . .<br>van Heugten (2013)<br>stated that . . .<br>or<br>The design is simple and pragmatic (Butler & Gardiner, 2019). Personal resilience is one factor that . . . (van Heugten, 2013). |

## MAGAZINE ARTICLE (FROM THE INTERNET)

| | |
|---|---|
| Reference list | Mehta, A. (2019, May). Beyond recycling: Putting the brakes on fast fashion. *Ethical Corporation.* https://events.ethicalcorp.com/reports/docs/548965/EC-Magazine- May-2019.pdf<br>Note: When a magazine or journal does not have volume or issue numbers the publication date e.g. (2019, May) becomes the issue information used to locate the article.<br>Replace the URL with a DOI, if one is available, at the end of the reference. Add https://doi.org/ *before the DOI number.* |
| In-text citation | Mehta (2019) stated that fashion trends . . . or<br>. . . these new attitudes may help control fashion consumption (Mehta, 2019). |

## ARCHIVED JOURNAL ARTICLE (FROM LIBRARY DATABASE)

| | |
|---|---|
| Reference list | *When an archived work is only available from one database, include the name of the database e.g. JSTOR. Provide the URL of the database homepage when there is no DOI.*<br>Bunkers, E., & Cochrane, W. (1957). On the income elasticity of food services. *The Review of Economics and Statistics, 39*(2), 211-217. JSTOR. https://doi.org/10.2307/1928539<br>Burk, M. (1951). Changes in the demand for food from 1941 to 1950. *Journal of Farm Economics, 33*(3), 281-298. JSTOR. https://www.jstor.org/ |
| In-text citation | Bunkers and Cochrane (1957) showed that in the long term demand for food . . . Burk (1951) had revealed that . . .<br>or<br>Demand had increased as a result . . . (Bunkers & Cochrane, 1957). The demand for food . . . (Burk, 1951). |

## ARCHIVED NON-ENGLISH JOURNAL ARTICLE TRANSLATED INTO ENGLISH (FROM A DATABASE)

| | |
|---|---|
| Reference list | *When an archived work is only available from one database, include the name of the database e.g. JSTOR.*<br>von der Luhe, I. (1982). I without guarantees: Ingeborg Bachmann's Frankfurt lectures on poetics (M. T. Kraus, Trans.). *New German Critique, 8*(27), 31- 56. JSTOR. https://doi.org/10.2307/487983<br>Note: When there is no DOI, provide the URL of the database homepage. |
| In-text citation | von der Luhe (1982) concludes that both states are essential. or<br>. . . that both states are essential (von der Luhe, 1982). |

## NEWSPAPER ARTICLE (VIA PRINT OR LIBRARY DATABASE)

| | |
|---|---|
| Reference list | *In most cases, a URL/ database name is not required. The reference will appear the same as for print.*<br>Berkovic, N. (2009, March 31). Handouts may not be sent: Tax office seeks quick resolution of High Court challenge. *The Australian*, p. 5. |
| In-text citation | Berkovic (2009)<br>explained that handouts . . .<br>or<br>It was suggested that handouts may not be sent (Berkovic, 2009). |

## NEWSPAPER ARTICLE (FROM THE INTERNET)

| | |
|---|---|
| Reference list | Griffis, D. (2019, November 21). In traditional language, there is no word for disability. *The Guardian.* https://www.theguardian.com/commentisfree/2019/nov/21/in- traditional-language-there-is-no-word-for-disability<br>*See also Webpage on a news website.* |
| In-text citation | Griffis (2019)<br>explained that<br>. . . or<br>It was suggested that meeting the needs of First Peoples . . . (Griffis, 2019). |

## ARCHIVED NEWSPAPER ARTICLE (FROM LIBRARY DATABASE)

| | |
|---|---|
| Reference list | *When access to an archived work is restricted to one database, include the name of the database e.g. Sydney Morning Herald Archives.*<br>Provide the URL of the database homepage when there is no DOI.<br>Wentworth, W. C. (1984, January 24). Why we need a permanent base on the moon. *The Sydney Morning Herald,* p. 11. Sydney Morning Herald Archives. http://archives.smh.com.au/index.php<br>Note : When there is no DOI, provide the URL of the database homepage. |
| In-text citation | Wentworth<br>(1984) stated<br>that . . . or<br>. . . the engineered apple (Wentworth, 1984). |

## PROCEEDINGS OF MEETINGS AND SYMPOSIUMS, CONFERENCE PAPERS

| Reference list | **Symposium contribution:**<br>Muelbauer, J. (2007, August 30–September 1). Housing, credit, and consumer expenditure. In S. C. Ludvigson (Chair), *Housing, Housing Finance, and Monetary Policy* [Symposium]. Economic Symposium Conference, Jackson Hole, WY, United States. https://bit.ly/2O4i6AY<br>**Conference session:**<br>Fulljames, T. (2009, July 9-10). *A career in tertiary management – a transformative experience!* [Paper presentation]. ATEM Aotearoa Conference, Christchurch, New Zealand. https://bit.ly/2Gbd0hG<br>Note: Conference proceedings published in a journal or book follow the same format as a journal article, edited book or edited book chapter. See pages 332-33 of the Publication Manual of the American Psychological Association (7th ed) for more examples. |
|---|---|
| In-text citation | Muelbauer<br>(2007) stated<br>that . . . or<br>It has been found that . . . (Muelbauer, 2007). |

## SYSTEMATIC REVIEWS

| Reference list | Osborn, D. A., & Sinn, J. K. H. (2006). Soy formula for prevention of allergy and food intolerance in infants. *Cochrane Database of Systematic Reviews.*<br>https://doi.org/10.1002/14651858.CD003741.pub4 |
|---|---|
| In-text citation | Osborn and Sinn<br>(2006) stated that<br>. . . or<br>It has been found that . . . (Osborn & Sinn, 2006) |

## OTHER MATERIALS

## AUDIO RECORDING

Use descriptors such as [Song], [Album]. For online audio see Podcast Episode example.

| | |
|---|---|
| Reference list | *For a classical work, provide the composer as author and the individual or group who recorded the work in square brackets after the title.*<br>Beethoven, L. van. (2020) Grosse fuge in B-flat major, op. 133. [Song recorded by Fine Arts Quartet]. On *Beethoven: Fuges and rarities for string quartet.* Naxos. (Original work published 1827)<br>*For all other recordings, provide the name of the recording artist or group as the author.*<br>Handel, A., & Seiler, G. L. (2006). Adoration [Song]. On *Ghosts and angels*. Feral Media.<br>*If a song has no associated album, add the name of the label after the descriptor [Song].*<br>Tame Impala. (2019). Patience. [Song]. Modular Recordings.<br>*To cite a whole album of recordings, use the word "Album" in square brackets after the title followed by a period.*<br>Jackson, J. (1979). Look Sharp [Album]. A&M Records.<br>Note: If the song or album is only available online, a URL can be added to the end of the reference.<br>For further examples see Publication Manual of the American Psychological Association (7th ed) section 10.13. |
| In-text citation | Handel and Seiler's (2006) track entitled "Adoration" combines . . . or<br>Classical and electronic styles have been combined . . . (Handel & Seiler, 2006). |

## AUSTRALIAN BUREAU OF STATISTICS

| | |
|---|---|
| Reference list | Australian Bureau of Statistics. (2000, November). *Use of the internet by householders, Australia* (no. 8147.0). https://www.abs.gov.au/ausstats/abs@.nsf/productsbytopic/AE8E67619446DB22CA2568A9001393F8?OpenDocument<br>Note: When the author is also the publishing body omit the publisher element. |
| In-text citation | The Australian Bureau of Statistics (2000) found that . . . or<br>. . . was shown in the census information (Australian Bureau of Statistics, 2000). |

## BROCHURE

| | |
|---|---|
| Reference list | Western Sydney University. (2016). *Transport access guide: Penrith Campus* [Brochure]. |
| In-text citation | Buses run on a schedule . . . (Western Sydney University, 2016). or<br>The Western Sydney University transport brochure (2016) shows that . . . |

## REPORT (ONLINE)

| | |
|---|---|
| Reference list | **Government report with group author:**<br>Department of Health and Ageing. (2008). *Ageing and aged care in Australia* (Publication No. P3-4147). http://www.health.gov.au/internet/main/publishing.nsf/Content/BFE46F21A3241ECBCA2574BE001A6E06/$File/Ageing_and_Aged_Care.pdf<br>When the author is also the publishing body omit the publisher element.<br>**Non-government report with individual authors:**<br>Este, J., Warren, C., Connor, L., Brown, M., Pollard, R., & O'Connor, T. (2008).<br>*Life in the clickstream: The future of journalism.* Media Entertainment and Arts Alliance.<br>http://www.alliance.org.au/documents/foj_report_final.pdf<br>Note: Reports in APA 7 belong to the grey literature reference category. For more examples see section 10.4 in the Publication Manual of the American Psychological Association (7th ed). |
| In-text citation | The Department of Health and Ageing<br>(2008) reported that... Este et al. (2008)<br>suggest that...<br>or<br>...was shown in the report (Department of Health and Ageing, 2008).<br>...it is necessary to develop... (Este et al., 2008). |

## IMAGE ON THE INTERNET

| | |
|---|---|
| Reference list | *An offering to the ocean in La Punta, Peru* [photograph]. (2009, May 19). http://www.smh.com.au/snapshots/<br>Frith, J. (1968, April 2). *It's on again* [Political cartoon]. Museum of Democracy Old Parliament House. https://frith.moadoph.gov.au/the-cartoons/14- it-s-on-again/<br>*Note: Other descriptors can be used in square brackets after the title as they apply to the image e.g.* Painting, Infographic, Clip art, Map. |
| In-text citation | In the above image (*An offering to the ocean in La Punta, Peru*, 2009) it can be seen...<br>Frith (1968) illustrates through his artwork . . . or<br>The cartoon (Frith, 1968) clearly shows the tension between political parties...<br>*An Offering to the Ocean in La Punta, Peru* (2009) shows...<br>Note: Use title case (capital letters for the main words) when using a title in-text. |

## LECTURE (UNPUBLISHED) / PERSONAL COMMUNICATION

| | |
|---|---|
| Reference list | *Note: When you cite information spoken about in a lecture that has gone unpublished, it is treated as a personal communication and you do not need to provide a reference list entry because there is no recoverable data. All details are provided in the text.*<br>*It is advisable to consider using published sources before using class/lecture notes as references in your paper.* |
| In-text citation | H. Dwyer (personal communication, January 10, 2009) discussed the . . . or<br>. . . found that in these cases "neutrons are dangerous" (H. Dwyer, personal communication, January 10, 2009). |

## PODCAST EPISODE (FROM THE INTERNET)

| | |
|---|---|
| Reference list | Atkin, M. (Host). (2008, November 13). Bermagui forest disputed turf [Audio podcast episode]. In *The hack half hour.* ABC.<br>https://www.abc.net.au/triplej/hack/notes/ |
| In-text citation | Atkin<br>(2008)<br>found that<br>. . . or<br>It was found . . . (Atkin, 2008). |

## THESIS

| | |
|---|---|
| Reference list | **Published:**<br>Fayadh, K. H. (2015). *The legal regulation of assisted reproductive technology in Iraq: Lessons from the Australian approach* [Doctoral dissertation, Western Sydney University]. Research Direct. http://handle.uws.edu.au:8081/1959.7/uws:32383<br>**Unpublished:**<br>Smith, D. (1958). *Change and continuity. Following the yellow brick road*<br>[Unpublished doctoral dissertation]. University of Oz.<br>Note: In Australia, a doctoral dissertation is also known as a PhD thesis. |
| In-text citation | Fayadh<br>(2015)<br>showed that<br>. . . or<br>It was found . . . (Fayadh, 2015). |

## VIDEO RECORDING, TELEVISION BROADCAST OR EPISODE IN A SERIES

Use descriptors such as [Film], [TV series], [TV series episode].

| | |
|---|---|
| Reference list | Hall, B. (Writer), & Bender, J. (Director). (1991, October 15). Rules of the game (Season 1, Episode 3) [TV series episode]. In J. Falsey (Executive Producer), *I'll fly away*. Brand-Falsey Productions; Lorimar Television.<br>Note: When there are multiple production companies, list them all and separate each company with a semi colon at the end of the reference. |
| In-text citation | Hall and Bender (1991)<br>examined the rules . . . or<br>The rules . . . (Hall & Bender, 1991). |

## VIDEO (FROM THE INTERNET)

| | |
|---|---|
| Reference list | Norton, R. (2006, November 4). *How to train a cat to operate a light switch* [Video]. YouTube. http://www.youtube.com/watch?v= Vja83KLQXZs |
| In-text citation | Norton (2006) showed that a cat<br>can be trained . . . or<br>Training a cat requires . . . (Norton, 2006). |

## WEBPAGES AND WEBSITES

When referencing webpages include the following elements:

- Author/editor/compiler
- Date
- Title
- Name of website (if not named as the author)
- Retrieval date if the source could change over time e.g. Facebook page, Twitter profile.
- URL

## WEBPAGE ON A NEWS WEBSITE

| | |
|---|---|
| Reference list | Scherer, J., & Lal, S. (2020, January 10). *Tourism industry suffers as bushfire images scare off international travellers*. SBS News. https://www.sbs.com.au/news/tourism-industry-suffers-as-bushfire- images-scare-off-international-travellers |
| In-text citation | Scherer and Lal<br>(2020) reported<br>. . . or<br>Reporting of disasters can affect local tourism (Scherer & Lal, 2020). |

## WEBPAGE ON THE INTERNET, ORGANISATION AS AUTHOR

| | |
|---|---|
| Reference list | SANE Australia. (2019). *What is mental illness?* https://www.sane.org/information-stories/facts-and-guides/what-is- mental-illness<br>Note: When the author and website name are the same omit the site name from the source element. Enter the group name as it appears on the website. |
| In-text citation | SANE Australia<br>(2019) explains that<br>. . . or<br>Mental illness is . . . (SANE Australia, 2019). |

## WEBPAGE ON A WEBSITE, INDIVIDUAL AUTHOR

| | |
|---|---|
| Reference list | Cooper, D. (2009, March 31). *Native ant may stop toad in its tracks.* ABC Science.<br>https://ab.co/2TteHPE |
| In-text citation | Cooper (2009) stated that<br>a ferocious ant . . . or<br>Meat ants may be able to help control toad numbers (Cooper, 2009). |

## WEBPAGE ON A WEBSITE, NO DATE

| | |
|---|---|
| Reference list | ACOSS & UNSW Sydney. (n.d.). *What is poverty?* Poverty and Inequality. http://povertyandinequality.acoss.org.au/poverty/<br>Note: (n.d.) = no date. Always include details of authorship or publication date when available. Carefully consider the reliability and authority of websites with no author and/or no date before including it as a reference. Enter group names as they appear on the website. |
| In-text citation | ACOSS and UNSW Sydney (n.d.) are joint researchers . . . or<br>Poverty in Australia is attributed to . . . (ACOSS & UNSW Sydney, n.d.). |

## WEBPAGE ON A WEBSITE, CONTENT LIKELY TO CHANGE

| | |
|---|---|
| Reference list | NSW Government Health. (n.d.). *NSW Health organisation chart*. Retrieved January 24, 2020, from https://www.health.nsw.gov.au/about/nswhealth/Pages/chart.aspx<br>Use 'Retrieved' and include a retrieval date only when the content on the website is likely to change and there is no access to archived content. An example might be a free online dictionary entry.<br>Note: When the author and website name are the same omit the site name from the source element. |
| In-text citation | NSW Government Health (n.d.) has implemented . . . or<br>Government bodies have been given the task . . . (NSW Government Health, n.d.). |

## WEBSITE

| | |
|---|---|
| Reference list | *When referring to a whole website a reference list entry and in-text citation is not required. Include the name of the website in-text and provide the URL in parentheses*<br>*For more information on referencing websites and webpages see Publication Manual of the American Psychological Association (7th ed) section 10.6 and the* APA Style website. |
| In-text | The Immigration and Citizenship website (https://immi.homeaffairs.gov.au/) is a good source of information for . . . |

## ONLINE SOCIAL MEDIA

| | |
|---|---|
| Reference list | **Facebook page:**<br>Western Sydney U-Hawkesbury Institute for the Environment. (n.d.). *Home* [Facebook page]. Facebook. Retrieved January 8, 2020, from https://www.facebook.com/westsyduhie<br>*Use 'Retrieved' and include a retrieval date only when the content on the website is likely to change and there is no access to archived content. e.g. Twitter profile or Facebook page.*<br>**Facebook post:**<br>Western Sydney U-Hawkesbury Institute for the Environment. (2018, November 12). *The importance of pollination* [Video]. Facebook. https://www.facebook.com/westsyduhie/videos/340203470100137/<br>Note: When the post is dated, a retrieval date is not required. |
| In-text citation | (Western Sydney U-Hawkesbury Institute for the Environment, n.d.) (Western Sydney U-Hawkesbury Institute for the Environment, 2018) or<br>Western Sydney U-Hawkesbury Institute for the Environment (n.d.)<br>Western Sydney U-Hawkesbury Institute for the Environment (2018) |

## REFERENCE LIST

In APA reference lists are prepared according to the alphabetical order of authors. If two authors have the same name then their initials are alphabetized. Punctuation is most important in reference lists. Each author is separated from the other author by a comma (,) there is a full stop (.) after each initial. Before the final author ampersand (&) is used. Put full stop (.) and space after bracketed date (2010). Colon between title and subtitle, space after colon but not before and title is given in italics, semicolon between publishers.

## MLA STYLE (https://library.westernsydney.edu.au/main/sites/default/files/pdf/cite_MLA.pdf)

The Modern Language Association Style (MLA) has been devised by the Modern Language Association of America. It's used for documentations in language and literature. In order to document as per MLA style the information about the sources has to be collected. Who is the author, title of the source, how was the source published, where do you find the source, and when was it published.

MLA format follows the author-page method of in-text citation. This means that the author's last name and the page number(s) from which the quotation or paraphrase is taken must appear in the text, and a complete reference should appear on your Works Cited page. The author's name may appear either in the sentence itself or in parentheses following the quotation or paraphrase, but the page number(s) should always appear in the parentheses, not in the text of your sentence. For example:

"The health programs should start before the rainy season in Kerala" (26). There is a tendency for spread of diseases during this season (Ramesh 26). Both these In-text citations direct the readers to the source.

## BOOKS AND BOOK CHAPTERS

### SINGLE AUTHOR

| | |
|---|---|
| Works Cited list | Andreasen, Nancy C. *Brave New Brain: Conquering Mental Illness in the Era of the Genome*. Oxford UP, 2001.<br>Note: If a book has a significant number of illustrations and their participation is important to your research you may wish to give the illustrator's name after the title. The same format applies for translators, editors etc. Give the name in the form as seen of the title page:<br>...*of the Genome*. Illustrated by Shirley Harland. ...<br>*To reference a single image see Image from a Book.* |
| In-text citation | Andreasen stated that...(56). Or<br>It is suggested that... (Andreasen 56). |

### TWO AUTHORS

| | |
|---|---|
| Works Cited list | Copstead, Lee Ellen, and Jacqueline L. Banasik. *Pathophysiology*. 5thed., Elsevier, 2013.<br>Note: Within each entry, author names should be listed in the order in which they appear on the source or as displayed on the title page |
| In-text citation | Copstead and<br>Banasik explains...<br>(26). or<br>...and therefore... (Copstead and Banasik 26). |

### THREE OR MORE AUTHORS

| | |
|---|---|
| Works Cited list | Schneider, Zevia, et al. *Nursing and Midwifery Research: Methods and Appraisal for Evidence-Based Practice*. 3rd ed., Elsevier Australia, 2007. |
| In-text citation | Schneider et al.<br>showed that ...<br>(72). or<br>...is demonstrated (Schneider et al. 72). |

## NO AUTHOR (INCL. DICTIONARY OR ENCYCLOPAEDIA)

| | |
|---|---|
| Works Cited list | *Guide to Agricultural Meteorological Practices*. 2nd ed., Secretariat of the World Meteorological Organization, 1981.<br>Note: For an authored dictionary/encyclopaedia, treat the source as an authored book. |
| In-text citation | The *Guide to Agricultural Meteorological Practices* provides… (17). or<br>This can be shown by… (*Guide* 17).<br>Note: To shorten a title in parentheses, always include the first word by which the source is alphabetically listed in the Works Cited list. Use a noun phrase if it is at the beginning of the title. |

## CORPORATE AUTHOR

| | |
|---|---|
| Works Cited list | Institute of Chartered Accountants in Australia. *AASB Standards for 2005: Equivalents to IFRSs as at August 2004*. Pearson Education, 2004. |
| In-text citation | According to the Institute of Chartered Accountants in Australia figures… (3). or<br>This can be seen to… (Institute of Chartered Accountants in Australia 3).<br>Note: Only terms that are commonly abbreviated can be used to shorten a corporate author in a parenthetical citation e.g. Department or Labour (Dept. of Labour) or Western Sydney University (Western Sydney U) |

## EDITED BOOK

| | |
|---|---|
| Works Cited list | Craven, Ian, editor. *Australian Cinema in the 1990s.* Frank Cass, 2001.<br>Note: For two or more editors use 'editors'. |
| In-text citation | Craven discussed the successful...(6). or<br>The film starred actors...(Craven 6). |

## CHAPTER OR ARTICLE IN BOOK

| | |
|---|---|
| Works Cited list | Knowles, Malcolm S. "Independent Study." *Using Learning Contracts,* Jossey-Bass, 1986, pp. 89-120.<br>*Note: You do not need to specify the chapter names from a book that is written in its entirety by the same authors, however if you wish to emphasise the use of one chapter it would be given in the above format. Page numbers are not required, however providing these can assist your reader to locate the source of your information.* |
| In-text citation | Knowles demonstrated that...(45). or<br>This study showed...(Knowles 45) |

## CHAPTER OR ARTICLE IN AN EDITED BOOK

| | |
|---|---|
| Works Cited list | Ferres, Kay. "Idiot Box: Television, Urban Myths and Ethical Scenarios." *Australian Cinema in the 1990s,* edited by Ian Craven, Frank Cass, 2001, pp. 175-88. |
| In-text citation | Ferres discussed the television episode... (45). or<br>The television episode...(Ferres 45). |

## E-BOOK

| | |
|---|---|
| Works Cited list | Gunaratne, Manjriker, editor. *The Foundation of Engineering Handbook*. CRC Press, 2013. *Taylor and Francis E books*, doi: 10.1201/b15592.<br>Mullan, John. *How Novels Work*. Oxford UP, 2006. *Proquest Ebook Central*, ebookcentral.proquest.com/lib/uwsau/detail.action?docID=834760.<br>Note: A URL is not required if a DOI is available. Add it to the end of the reference. If the book was accessed through a database, include a stable URL (also known as a permalink, bookmark or embedded link) after the database name. If you provide a URL omit http:// or https://. |
| In-text citation | Mullan stated that...(40). ...Gunaratne presents a critical...50. or<br>Narration is... (Mullan 40). ...handbooks that analyse...(Gunaratne 50). |

## JOURNAL ARTICLES, NEWSPAPER ARTICLES AND CONFERENCE PAPERS

The format for more than one author is the same for all sources including journal articles, therefore, refer to the examples for books in this guide.

## JOURNAL ARTICLE (PRINT VERSION)

| | |
|---|---|
| Works Cited list | Younger, P[aula]. "Using the Internet to Conduct a Literature Search." *Nursing Standard,* vol. 19, no.6, 2004, pp. 45-51.<br>Note: If the full name of the author is known but not given on the title page it can be added within square brackets. |
| In-text citation | Younger stated that the... (46). or<br>The Internet can be used to conduct a literature search (Younger 46). |

## JOURNAL ARTICLE (FULL-TEXT FROM ELECTRONIC DATABASE)

| Works Cited list | Jackson, Debra, et al. "Personal Resilience as a Strategy for Surviving and Thriving in the Face of Workplace Adversity: A Literature Review." *Journal of Advanced Nursing*, vol. 60, no. 1, 2007, pp. 1-9. *Academic Search Complete, EBSCOHost*, doi: 10.1111/j.1365-2648.2007.04412.x.<br>Note: If a DOI number is available for the journal article, include it at the end of the Works Cited. |
|---|---|
| In-text citation | Jackson et al. found that... (7). or<br>...a useful strategy (Jackson et al. 7). |

## NEWSPAPER ARTICLE (AVAILABLE IN PRINT)

| Works Cited list | Berkovic, Nicola. "Handouts May Not Be Sent: Tax Office Seeks Quick Resolution of High Court Challenge." *The Australian*, 31 Mar. 2009, p. 5.<br>Note: If the article is separated across non-consecutive pages, give the first page number followed by a plus sign, leaving no intervening space e.g. pp. 5+.<br>If a section name is required it is given as follows:<br>...Apr. 2009, Travel sec, p. 6. |
|---|---|
| In-text citation | Berkovic explained that handouts... (5). or<br>It was suggested that handouts may not be sent (Berkovic 5). |

## NEWSPAPER ARTICLE (FROM ELECTRONIC DATABASE)

| Works Cited list | Wentworth, W.C. "Why We Need a Permanent Base on the Moon." *Sydney Morning Herald*, 24 Jan. 1984, p. 11. *Sydney Morning Herald Archives*, ezproxy.uws.edu.au/login?url=http://archives.smh.com.au/fnc_login_a.php |
|---|---|
| In-text citation | Wentworth stated that...(11). or<br>....and this demonstrates the need for a permanent base (Wentworth 11). |

## ARTICLE (FROM THE INTERNET)

| | |
|---|---|
| Works Cited list | Cooper, Dani. "Native Ant May Stop Toad in its Tracks." *ABC Science*, 31 Mar. 2009, www.abc.net. au/science/articles//2009/03/31/2530686.htm? site=science&topic=latest. |
| In-text citation | In a recent *ABC Science* article, Cooper stated that a ferocious ant... or<br>...the ants may be able to help control toad numbers (Cooper). |

## NON-ENGLISH JOURNAL ARTICLE TRANSLATED INTO ENGLISH

| | |
|---|---|
| Works Cited list | Von Der Luhe, Irmela. "I Without Guarantees: Ingeborg Bachmann's Frankfurt Lectures on Poetics.", translated by M. T. Kraus, *New German Critique*, vol. 8, no. 27, 1982, pp. 31-56. |
| In-text citation | Von Der Luhe concludes that... (35). or<br>...examines the poetics... (Von Der Luhe 35). |

## PROCEEDINGS OF MEETINGS AND SYMPOSIUMS

| | |
|---|---|
| Works Cited list | Chang, Steve S., et al., editors. *Proceedings of the Twenty-Fifth Annual Meeting of the Berkeley Linguistics Society, February 12-15, 1999: General Session and Parasession on Loan Word Phenomena.* Berkeley Linguistics Society, 2000. |
| In-text citation | At the conference on loan word phenomena, Chang et al. stated that...(23). or<br>It has been found that...(Chang et al. 23). |

## CONFERENCE PROCEEDINGS (FROM ELECTRONIC DATABASE)

| | |
|---|---|
| Works Cited list | Bukowski, Ronald M. "Prognostic Factors for Survival in Metastatic Renal Cell Carcinoma: Update 2008. Innovations and Challenges in Renal Cancer: Proceedings of the Third Cambridge Conference." *Cancer*, vol. 115, no. 10, 2009, pp. 2273-2281. *Academic OneFile*, doi: 10.1002/cncr.24226.<br>Note: When conference proceedings are published as an article in a journal use double quotation marks around the title. |
| In-text citation | Bukowski stated that...(2274). or<br>It has been found that...(Bukowski 2274) |

## OTHER MATERIALS

### AUSTRALIAN BUREAU OF STATISTICS

| | |
|---|---|
| Works Cited list | *Use of the Internet by Householders, Australia.* Cat. no. 8147.0, Australian Bureau of Statistics, Nov. 2000, www.abs.gov.au/AUSSTATS/abs@.nsf/7d12b0f6763c78caca257061001cc588/ae8e67619446db22ca2568a9001393f8!Open Document.<br>Note: When an organisation is both the author and the publisher, skip the author element and begin the entry with the title then include the organisation as the publisher. |
| In-text citation | *Use of the Internet by Householders, Australia* found that... or<br>...was shown in the census information (*Use*).<br>Note: If the title that is placed in parentheses does not begin with a noun phrase, provide the first word in the title if this is enough to direct the reader to the entry in the Works Cited list. For further information, see 3.2.1 in the MLA Handbook (8th edition). |

## BROCHURE

| | |
|---|---|
| Works Cited list | *Transport Access Guide: Penrith Campus.* Western Sydney U, 2009. |
| In-text citation | Buses run on a schedule…(*Transport Access Guide*) or<br>The Western Sydney University *Transport Access Guide* for the Penrith campus shows that… |

## GOVERNMENT REPORT (ONLINE)

| | |
|---|---|
| Works Cited list | *Ageing and Aged Care in Australia.* Department of Health and Ageing, Australian Government, 2008, www.health.gov.au/internet/main/publishing.nsf/ Content/ageing.<br>Where organisations are both the author and publisher, skip the author element. Where a government agency is the author but not the publisher begin the entry with the name of the government followed by a comma and name of the agency e.g. Australian Government, Department of Health and Ageing… |
| In-text citation | The report *Ageing and Aged Care in Australia* reported that… or<br>…was shown in the report (*Ageing*). |

## IMAGE FROM A BOOK (OR OTHER MEDIA)

| | |
|---|---|
| Works Cited list | Tschichold, Jan. "Die Frau Ohne Namen." (The Woman without a Name). 1927.<br>*Clean New World: Culture, Politics, and Graphic Design,* MIT P, 2001, p. 32. Offset lithograph poster.<br>Note: A description of the source can be added at the end of the Works Cited entry if clarity is needed. |
| In-text citation | In Tschichold's artwork "Frau Ohne Namen" it can be seen… (32). or<br>"Frau Ohne Namen" shows…(Tschichold 32). |

## IMAGE ON THE INTERNET

| | |
|---|---|
| Works Cited list | "An Offering to the Ocean in La Punta, Peru." *Sydney Morning Herald*, 19 May. 2009, www.smh.com.au/snapshots/. Web Image. |
| In-text citation | In the photograph ("Offering") it can be seen… or "An Offering to the Ocean in La Punta, Peru", pictured below, shows… A title that is not in parentheses may be abbreviated after the first in text citation |

## LECTURE (UNPUBLISHED) / PERSONAL COMMUNICATION

| | |
|---|---|
| Works Cited list | Elliott, K. "Neutrons." Protons and Neutrons, 6 Jul. 2015, Western Sydney U. Lecture. |
| In-text citation | …found that neutrons… (Elliot) or In her 2015 lecture, Elliott discussed neutrons and… |

## PODCAST (FROM THE INTERNET)

| | |
|---|---|
| Works Cited list | Atkin, Michael, reporter. "Bermagui Forest Disputed Turf." *The Hack Half Hour*, ABC, 13 Nov. 2008, www.abc.net.au/triplej/hack/notes/. Podcast. |
| In-text citation | Atkin found that… or It was found…(Atkin). |

## THESIS / DISSERTATION (ONLINE)

| | |
|---|---|
| Works Cited list | Fayadh, Khaled H. *The Legal Regulation of Assisted Reproductive Technology in Iraq: Lessons from the Australian Approach*. Western Sydney U, 2015, handle.uws.edu.au:8081/1959.7/uws:32383. PhD thesis. |
| In-text citation | Fayadh showed that…(11-12). or It was found…(Fayadh 11-12). |

## VIDEO RECORDING, TELEVISION PROGRAM OR AUDIO RECORDING

Use descriptors such as video recording, television episode or audio recording

| | |
|---|---|
| Works Cited list | "Rules of the Game." *I'll Fly Away* New York Broadcasting Company, 1991. Television episode. |
| In-text citation | The 1991 episode "Rules of the game" showed the... or The episode could be described as... ("Rules"). |

## VIDEO OR AUDIO (FROM THE INTERNET)

| | |
|---|---|
| Works Cited list | Norton, R. *How to Train a Cat to Operate a Light Switch.* 4 Nov. 2006, www.youtube.com/watch?v= Vja83KLQXZs. Online video. |
| In-text citation | In the video posted to YouTube, Norton showed that a cat can be trained... or Training a cat requires...(Norton). |

WEB PAGE / DOCUMENT ON THE INTERNET

| Works Cited list | Document on the Internet:<br>Este, Jonathan, et al. *Life in the Clickstream: The Future of Journalism*. Media Entertainment and Arts Alliance, 2008, www.alliance.org.au/documents/foj_report_final.pdf.<br>Document on the Internet, no author, no date:<br>*Developing an Argument*. Princeton Writing Center, web.princeton.edu/sites/ Writing/Writing_Center/WCWritingResources.htm. Accessed 13 April 2017.<br>Note: If the source does not include a publication date, omit the date and include an access date at the end of the Works Cited entry.<br>If you have found the date from a reliable external source, place the date in square brackets to show that the information did not come from the source. If there is uncertainty about the publication date provided, include a question mark after the date. For further information, refer to 2.6.1 in the MLA Handbook (8th edition).<br>Always include details of authorship and publication date when available. For websites with no author and/or date, carefully consider the reliability and authority of the source before including it as a reference. |
|---|---|
| In-text citation | In *Life in the Clickstream*, Este et al. suggest that... or<br>...it is necessary to develop an argument (*Developing*). |

## DIFFERENCE BETWEEN MLA &APA

There are certain differences and similarities between MLA style and APA style. It is briefly given in the following two tables.

| Differences | MLA | APA |
|---|---|---|
| Reference Page | In MLA, this page is labelled as "Works Cited" | In APA, this page is labelled as "References" |
| Order of Entries on Reference Page | References are arranged in alphabetical order by author's names first, then by title | References are first arranged in alphabetical order by author's names, then chronologically (oldest first) |
| Multiple Works by Same Author | Work is listed from newest to oldest, but the author's name is only mentioned in the first entry | List the works chronologically but include the author's name in each entry |
| Article Titles | Titles are referenced in quotation marks with major words capitalized | Only the first word of the title is capitalized; no quotation marks are used |
| In-Text Referencing | Write authors' names, then page number of the source being referenced | Write authors' names, then year that the source was published |

**(https://www.uopeople.edu/blog/apa-vs-mla-college-preference/)**

**Comparison of APA and MLA citation styles**

| | APA | MLA |
|---|---|---|
| General Format | Author's name / Date of publication / Title / Place of publication / Publisher. | Author's name / Title / Place of publication / Publisher / Date of publication. |
| Book | Kesey, K. (1962). *One Flew over the Cuckoo's Nest.* New York: Signet. | Kesey, Ken. *One Flew over the Cuckoo's Nest.* New York: Signet. 1962. |
| Article in a Book | Bunselmeyer, J.E. (2002). Faulkner's narrative styles. In L. Wagner-Martin (Ed.) William Faulkner: Six Decades of Criticism. (pp. 313-331). East Lansing. MI: Michigan State University Press. | Bunselmeyer, J.E. "Faulkner's Narrative Styles." William Faulkner: Six Decades of Criticism. Ed. L. Wagner-Martin. East Lansing. MI: Michigan State UP. 2002. 313-31. |
| Article in a Periodical | Devlin, K.J. (2006). The scopic drive and visual projection in Heart of Darkness. Modern Fiction Studies, 52 (1). 19-41. | Devlin, Kimberly J. "The Scopic Drive and Visual Projection in Heart of Darkness." Modern Fiction Studies 52.1 (2006): 19-41. |
| Newspaper / Magazine article | Garbacz, S. (2006, November 14). Experts discuss effects of binge drinking on careers. The Exponent, p. 1. | Garbacz, Steve. "Experts Discuss Effects of Binge Drinking on Careers." The Exponent 14 Nov. 2006: 1. |
| Web Source | Womack, M. (1997). Edgar Allan Poe's "The Black Cat". Retrieved November 16, 2006, from http://www.poedecoder.com/essays/blackcat/ | Womack, Martha. "Edgar Allan Poe's 'The Black Cat'." 1997. The Poe Decoder. 16 November 2006 <http://www.poedecoder.com/essays/blackcat/> |

**(https://www.pinterest.com/pin/303993662112331148//)**

## CHICAGO MANUAL (https://library.westernsydney.edu.au/main/sites/default/files/pdf/cite_Chicago.pdf)

Chicago Manual style is used for both the humanities and Social Sciences. It's a little complex compared to APA and MLA Styles. Chicago-style source citations come in two varieties: (1) notes and bibliography and (2) author-a little

.date. The guide specifically focuses on American English and deals with aspects of editorial practice, including grammar and usage, as well as document preparation and formatting. The latest edition is the 17th which came out in 2017.

## BOOKS AND BOOK CHAPTERS

### SINGLE AUTHOR

| | |
|---|---|
| Bibliography | Sylwester, Robert. *The Adolescent Brain: Reaching for Autonomy*. Heatherton, Victoria: Hawker Brownlow Education, 2008. |
| Footnote | 1. Sylwester, *Adolescent Brain*, 89. |

### TWO OR THREE AUTHORS

| | |
|---|---|
| Bibliography | Anderson, Jonathan, and Millicent E. Poole. *Assignment and Thesis Writing*. 4th ed. Milton, Qld.: John Wiley & Sons, 2001. |
| Footnote | 2. Anderson and Poole, *Assignment and Thesis Writing*, 65. |

### FOUR OR MORE AUTHORS

| | |
|---|---|
| Bibliography | Hansen, Anders, Simon Cottle, Ralph Negrine, and Chris Newbold. *Mass Communication Research Methods*. Basingstoke: Macmillan, 1998.<br>Note: Invert only the first author's name e.g. surname, first name. |
| Footnote | 3. Anders et al., *Mass Communication Research Methods*, 104.<br>*Note: In the footnote, if an item has more than three authors you may abbreviate the remaining authors as '*et al.*' ("and others").* |

## NO AUTHOR (INCL. DICTIONARY OR ENCYCLOPEDIA)

| | |
|---|---|
| Bibliography | *Merriam-Webster's Collegiate Dictionary.* 10th ed. Springfield, MA: Merriam Webster, 1993. |
| Footnote | 4. *Merriam-Webster's*, 11. |

## EDITED BOOK

| | |
|---|---|
| Bibliography | Craven, Ian, ed. *Australian Cinema in the 1990s.* London: Frank Cass, 2001. |
| Footnote | 5. Craven, *Australian Cinema*, 25. |

## CHAPTER OR ARTICLE IN BOOK

| | |
|---|---|
| Bibliography | Knowles, Malcolm S. "Independent Study." In *Using Learning Contracts*, 73-112. San Francisco: Jossey-Bass, 1986. |
| Footnote | 6. Knowles, "Independent Study," 79. |

## CHAPTER OR ARTICLE IN AN EDITED BOOK

| | |
|---|---|
| Bibliography | Ferres, Kay. "Idiotbox: Television, Urban Myths and Ethical Scenarios." In *Australian Cinema in the 1990s*, edited by Ian Craven, 175-88. London: Frank Cass, 2001.<br>See also CMOS section 14.108 on how to cite several contributions by different authors from the same book. |
| Footnote | 7. Ferres, "Idiot Box," 179. |

E-BOOK

| | |
|---|---|
| Bibliography | Mullan, John. *How Novels Work*. Oxford: OUP, 2006. ProQuest Ebook Central.<br>If a DOI is available, include it as a URL at the end of the reference, e.g. https://doi.org/10.1086/884652. If there is no DOI and the book is accessed via a library database, add the name of the database. If the e-book has no DOI and not available via a library database add the URL at the end. |
| Footnote | 8. Mullan, *How Novels Work*, chap. 2, Recollections.<br>*When a work is not paginated use chapter or paragraph number (if available) section heading or descriptive phrase. If the document is small and searchable, locators may be omitted. For more information on page location in electronic format and online see CMOS* sections *14.160 and 14.161.* |

## JOURNAL ARTICLES, NEWSPAPER ARTICLES AND CONFERENCE PAPERS

The format for more than one author is the same for all sources including journal articles, therefore, refer to the examples for books in this guide.

JOURNAL ARTICLE (PRINT VERSION)

| | |
|---|---|
| Bibliography | Younger, Paula. "Using the Internet to Conduct a Literature Search." *Nursing Standard* 19, no. 6 (2004): 45-51.<br>Chicago style only includes the issue number (e.g. no. 6) for special/theme issues, or where the pagination does not continue throughout the volume, i.e. starts from 1 in each issue. Month or issue date is preferred over issue number. |
| Footnote | 9. Younger, "Using the Internet," 45-47. |

## JOURNAL ARTICLE (FULL-TEXT FROM ELECTRONIC DATABASE)

| Bibliography | Jackson, Debra, Angela Firtko, and Michael Edenborough. "Personal Resilience as a Strategy for Surviving and Thriving in the Face of Workplace Adversity: A Literature Review." *Journal of Advanced Nursing* 60, no. 1 (2007): 1-9. https://doi.org/10.1111/j.1365-2648.2007.04412.x.<br>*If a DOI is available add the URL prefix* https://doi.org, *no further location elements are required. If no DOI is available, provide the name of the database or a stable URL.* |
|---|---|
| Footnote | 10. Jackson, Firkto and Edenborough, "Personal Resilience," 3. |

## NON-ENGLISH JOURNAL ARTICLE TRANSLATED INTO ENGLISH

| Bibliography | Von Der Luhe, I. "I Without Guarantees: Ingeborg Bachmann's Frankfurt Lectures on Poetics." Translated by MT Kraus. *New German Critique* 8, no. 27 (1982): 31-56. |
|---|---|
| Footnote | 11. Von Der Luhe, "I Without Guarantees," 36. |

## NEWSPAPER ARTICLE

| | |
|---|---|
| Bibliography | *Note: In the Chicago style, newspaper articles are more commonly cited in notes than in a Bibliography. Include all details in the footnote. Chicago does not recommend using page numbers for newspaper articles but a section number or edition could be included. For an article available on the internet, include the URL. If the online content is subject to change such as breaking news provide a time stamp and if instructed by your lecturer, an access date. e.g. …3:55 pm. EST, accessed July 27, 2014,* http://smh.com... |
| Footnote | 12. H. Berkovic, "Handouts May Not be Sent: Tax Office Seeks Quick Resolution of High Court Challenge," *Australian*, March 31, 2009.<br>7. Jason Samenow, "Storm Warning: High Winds," *Washington Post*, January 21, 2016, 3:55 p.m. EST, https://www.washingtonpost.com/news/capital-weather-gang/wp/2016/01/21/. |

## NEWSPAPER ARTICLE (FROM ELECTRONIC DATABASE)

| | |
|---|---|
| Bibliography | *Note: Newspaper articles are more commonly cited in notes than in the Bibliography. Include all details in the footnote. If a stable URL is not available use the name of the database instead. (for more examples see CMOS section 14.191 – 14.200).* |
| Footnote | 13. WC. Wentworth, "Why We Need a Permanent Base on the Moon,"<br>*Sydney Morning Herald*, January 24, 1984, Sydney Morning Herald Archives. |

## ARTICLE (FROM THE INTERNET)

| | |
|---|---|
| Bibliography | Cooper, D. "Native Ant May Stop Toad in its Tracks." *ABC Science*, March 31, 2009. http://www.abc.net.au/science/articles/2009/03/31/2530686.htm?site=science&topic=latest. |
| Footnote | 14. Cooper, "Native Ant". |

## PROCEEDINGS OF MEETINGS AND SYMPOSIUMS, CONFERENCE PAPERS

| | |
|---|---|
| Bibliography | Boardman, Margot. "Learning Communities Contribution to Educational Improvement: Joint Participation for Mutual Gain in Early Childhood Education." Paper presented at the *International Education Research Conference AARE/NZARE*, Auckland, New Zealand, November 30 - December 3, 2003. http://aare.edu.au/03pap/boa03496.pdf. |
| Footnote | 15. Boardman, "Learning Communities", 13. |

# OTHER MATERIALS

## INTERVIEW UNPUBLISHED/ PERSONAL COMMUNICATION

| | |
|---|---|
| Bibliography | *Unpublished interviews or personal communications are only cited in footnotes; they are not listed in Bibliographies. All details are provided in the footnote* |
| Footnote | Interview conducted by yourself:<br>1. Graham Strong (pastor, Wayfare Chapel), interview by author, May 5, 2014.<br>**Interview conducted by another person:**<br>2. Nellie Melba, interview by Albert Smith, September 1924, Oral History Archive, National Library, Australia.<br>**Personal email. Begin with the name of the sender:**<br>3. Graham Strong (pastor, Wayfare Chapel), email message to the author, May 23, 2014.<br>**If source is referred to again use the short form:**<br>7. Melba, interview. |

## ONLINE LECTURE / LECTURE NOTES

| | |
|---|---|
| Bibliography | *Avoid citing lectures where possible. It is better to go directly to the source. Ask your lecturer for a bibliography of their lecture or check your unit's Readings and Resources list.*<br>Lectures are only cited in footnotes; they are not listed in Bibliographies unless advised by your tutor or lecturer. |
| Footnote | **Face to face lecture:**<br>24. Stan Dyer, "Introduction" (lecture, 101033 Modernism, Western Sydney University, Penrith. January 10, 2014).<br>**Recorded lecture:**<br>26. Stan Dyer, "History of Modernism," lecture, 101033 Modernism, Western Sydney University, May 26, 2014, webinar, MPEG copy, 0:40:37, https://vuws.westernsydney.edu.au/webapps/blackboard/execute/handlle=lecture=vie<br>If the file can be downloaded provide the file name and length of recording. For lecture notes provide the file type e.g. PDF or PowerPoint after the title. |

## MUSIC SCORE

| | |
|---|---|
| Bibliography | Mozart, Wolfgang Amadeus. *Sonatas and Fantasies for the Piano*. Prepared from the autographs and earliest printed sources by Nathan Broder. Rev. Ed. Bryn Mawr, PA: Theodore Presser, 1960. |
| Footnote | 27. Mozart, *Sonatas and Fantasies.* |

## ARTICLE/CHAPTER FROM UNIT READER

| | |
|---|---|
| Bibliography | Rousseau, Jean-Jacques. "The Reveries of the Solitary Walker." In *Text and History 100598 Unit Reader.* Compiled by Annette Smith 33-46. Penrith: University Western Sydney, 2014. Originally published in Walter Kelly trans. and John Flinders ed., *The Collected Writings of Rousseau,* (London: George Pell & Sons, 1938).<br>If the work has come from the public domain e.g. public website, use the words ...<br>reprinted from Walter Kelly, ... *If original publication details are not provided then treat as a chapter in an edited book or consult your lecturer.* |
| Footnote | 31. Rousseau, "Reveries of the Solitary Walker", 35. |

## VIDEO (FROM] THE INTERNET)

| | |
|---|---|
| Bibliography | South Lanarkshire TV. "In Focus: Forest Kindergarten." YouTube video, 5:42.<br>August 13, 2010. https://www.youtube.com/watch?v=g8WWrRzf7ZU&list=TLEXvO6QPFaLk.<br>Cite non-conventional formats of author names and words e.g. YouTube as they appear in the source. 5:42 indicates the length of the video. |
| Footnote | 35. SouthLanarkshireTV, "In Focus: Forest Kindergarten." |

## AUDIO (FROM THE INTERNET)

| | |
|---|---|
| Bibliography | "Allegro Molto Appassionato," *Violin Concerto in E minor, Op. 64.* Performed by Franziska Früh (violin) with the Fulda Symphony Orchestra, Grosser Saal der Orangerie Fulda, March 18, 2001, 13 min., 27 sec. https:// commons. wikimedia.org/wiki/File:Felix_Mendelssohn Violinkonzert_e-moll_1._Allegro_molto_ appassionato.ogg.<br>*If the audio visual item is a downloadable file, include the format after the date before the URL or access date if one is used e.g.* ....November 4, 2006. MPEG, http://www...<br>The reference can be formatted under the title of the recording or the composer/performer depending on which is most important to the discussion.<br>For a database provide a stable URL or the name of the database e.g. Music Online. |
| Footnote | 36. "Allegro Molto Appassionato." |

## THESIS

| | |
|---|---|
| Bibliography | Fayadh, Khalad Hamad. "The legal regulation of assisted reproductive technology in Iraq: Lessons from the Australian approach." PhD thesis, Western Sydney University, 2015. http://handle.uws.edu.au:8081/1959.7/uws:32383.<br>A thesis is treated as not published or informally published therefore the title is not italicized |
| Footnote | 31. Fayadh, "Legal regulation," 6. |

## UNPUBLISHED WORKS OR DOCUMENTS (ARCHIVED MANUSCRIPTS OR LETTERS)

| | |
|---|---|
| Bibliography | *Note: Archived unpublished works such as manuscripts and letters are often stored in microform or in online databases. Add the format type and URL to the reference as required. Private documents are detailed only in the note if the sources are not retrievable as with personal communication.*<br>Matthews, Race. Letter and photographs from the Hon Race Mathews, MLA to Hon. E.G. Whitlam AC, QC, September 1, 1985. Accessed October 21, 2009. http://cem.uws.edu.au/R/YHLSR23PA4CH-00346?func=results-jump-full&set_entry=000005. |
| Footnote | 33. Matthews to Whitlam, 1 September 1985, Letter. |

## WEB PAGE / DOCUMENT ON THE INTERNET

| | |
|---|---|
| Bibliography | **Document on the internet:**<br>Este, J., C. Warren, L. Connor, M. Brown, R. Pollard and T. O'Connor. *Life in the Clickstream: The Future of Journalism*. Media Entertainment and Arts Alliance, 2008. http://www.alliance.org.au/documents/foj_report_final.pdf.<br>**Document on the internet, no author, no date:**<br>*Developing an argument.* Princeton Writing Centre. Accessed May 12, 2014. http://web.princeton.edu/sites/writing/Writing_Center/WCWritingResources.htm.<br>**Web page on the internet, no author no date:**<br>"Swim with Whales: An Unforgettable Wildlife Encounter." WDCS International. Accessed November 18, 2014. http://whales.org/encounters/big_whales.<br>When there is no publication or modified date use the access date. They may also be used if instructed by your academic in cases where websites are subject to change.<br>For further information and examples on webpages and websites see CMOS section 14.206 and 14.207. |
| Footnote | 37. Este et al., *Life in the Clickstream.*<br>38. *Developing an Argument.*<br>39. "Swim with whales." |

There are a lot of style manuals developed by different Universities and other institutions. The commonly used styles are discussed. Thousands of citation styles are there. These manuals help to order your writing and develop writing skills.

## REFERENCE MANAGEMENT SOFTWARE

References sources are authoritative works that help to locate information about people, facts or ideas. While attempting to write something, the author looks for such authoritative works and reads them to have a basic idea on the subject. It is most important to cite such works consulted. Earlier, style manuals were consulted for preparing citations within text and reference lists. Reference lists were prepared manually and switching from referencing styles was not easy. The advent of RMS relieved the scholars and writers of such cumbersome jobs of making and noting down their references. Reference management is one of the hardest jobs for preparing a research paper or any other academic writing. Organizing the important refer such works to get more credibility to their works citations and formatting. Earlier as per the style guides manually is a very difficult process. The reference management software can easily create citations and references and shift to whatever style within no time. The main functionalities of RMS are :

- Collect and organize information for your writing
- Extracts metadata from pdf files
- Work with word processing applications to facilitate In-text citation
- Produces a variety of citations in varied styles like APA, MLA, Harvard, etc
- Share data with research groups or communities
- Citations can be imported from bibliographic databases.

Fenner and Bartling (2014). RMS is a package that enables one to collect, organize, share, and use bibliographic references. The PDFs you may download for your study can be imported to your reference manager and can be used to read, bookmark, or highlight in text, or create and export citations. Searching and adding to the library is also possible. Reference Manager acts as a storage of your collections. These stored databases can be searched, indexed, and labeled. It can be organized in folders for each part.

## POPULAR REFERENCE MANAGEMENT TOOLS (SOFTWARE)

There are varieties of reference management software available. Prominent among are Endnote, Mendeley and Zotero.

### ENDNOTE

This is a proprietary reference management software of Clarivate Analytics. It is one of the best RMS with enhanced features and has been used by scientists and researchers for more than 20 years for organising their bibliographies, citations and references while working on an academic paper. Cite while you write option is available for word documents and one can easily shift from one referencing style to another in no time. PDFs can be imported to Endnote and a watch folder can be maintained to which the related files are automatically uploaded.If you have a desktop Endnote library open in your system, you can search a database for eg. Science Direct , and one the search results are displayed , select the boxes you want to export and export the article citations to your endnote library. One can add references manually to the endnote library. References can be grouped and these can be shared to other Endnote users also.

### MENDELEY

Mendeley was originally developed and owned by a start up firm during 2008. It offered a free package which can be upgraded for more features and storage space. Mendeley was taken over by Elsevier. Mendeley is a reference manager as well as an academic social network, which organises your files, shares with others, collaborates and it provides recommendations based on your interest. Mendeley has a citation plugin which can be installed in Ms Word or Libre Office Writer. This will enable one to insert In-text citation or Cite While you Write option. A web importer is also there which allows you to import a citation to mendeley account from a browser. Web importer can be installed for Firefox, Google Chrome or Safari browsers. Desktop and online versions of mendeley are available. You can work on the desktop version offline and sync while you are online. It acts as a pocket research tool. Mobile version can also be downloaded from playstore.

## ZOTERO

Zotero was developed in 2006 by George Mason University's Center for History and New Media. It is a free open source application software. Zotero desktop standalone is available, a plugin for firefox browser can be installed and on one click on the icon the citation is saved to your zotero account. Zotero automatically senses information from the web as per your research interest.

Cite This for me, Bibliography.com, Refworks etc., are other reference management applications. This software has made the referencing mechanism so simple and hurdle free. This is promoting fair use of resources by giving proper citations and credit for the respective authors. It makes writing more easy and systematic.

## REFERENCES

Fenner M., Scheliga K., Bartling S. (2014) Reference Management. In: Bartling S., Friesike S. (eds) Opening Science. Springer, Cham. https://doi.org/10.1007/978-3-319-00026-8_8

https://owll.massey.ac.nz/referencing/apa-reference-list.php

https://www.chicagomanualofstyle.org/home.html

# 5
# Citation Analysis and Information Metrics

Citation analysis deals with the mathematical analysis of bibliographic references. Two parties are dealt with in the analysis, the paper cited and the one who cites the particular paper. The analysis of these elements can give valuable information about the current and emerging knowledge on a subject. The number of times an article is cited the more it gains importance. Citation analysis helps a research administrator or anyone who wants to keep account of the authors or publications in a discipline. Citations are high in the field of science and those journals have very high impact. Citation analysis involves counting of the number of citations to a particular paper for a period of years after its publication. The number of years for which the citations are counted is known as the citation window which may vary from one field to another.

## CITATION INDEX

The first trace of citation index was found in the 12$^{th}$ century Hebrew religious literature. During 18$^{th}$ century Legal Citation Indexes were found. In 1960, Eugene Garfield's Institute for Scientific Information (ISI), introduced the first citation index for papers published in academic journals, the Science Citation Index. Later this was extended to Social Science Citation Indexes and Arts and Humanities Indexes. An automated indexing model was developed in 1997 called Citeseer. The 20th century saw many publishers brought out subscription-based citation indexes. Web of Science by Clarivate Analytics, Elsevier's SCOPUS are subscription based and CiteSeer and Google Scholar are free to use.

## TYPES OF CITATIONS

**Self-Citations:** "Self-citation may be said to occur when at least one of the authors of a cited document is the same person as one of the authors of the citing document. The author self-citation rate of an individual may be calculated by dividing the number of self-citations by the total number of all citations made by the individual". Self-citation may artificially inflate citation rate;

**Co-operational citations:** The cited author under study and one citing author were co-authors prior to the publication of cited paper and criterion (i) does not hold; and

**Independent citations:** No detectable relations between cited and citing author is observed.

## WHY CITATIONS?

Apart from the scientific merit there are other factors which influence the choice of references an author cites. It may be familiarity with particular papers or reputation of an author in a field, its availability or language, controversy of the topic, reprint dissemination, and coverage by secondary services etc. Papers more than 5 years old are cited less frequently, because these are superseded by books or reviews. Only a classic paper is cited when it is old. A well-known established author is more frequently cited than a new researcher in the field.

## RELATIVE ADVANTAGES OF CITATION ANALYSIS

- It's a tool in analysing research. Its helps to the trends in utilization of information author wise, subject wise, journal wise etc.,
- The relativity and interdependency of subjects can be known from citation analysis
- It studies the degree of scattering of literature
- Shows the life of documents
- For ranking journals eg. Journal Citation Reports
- For compiling reference lists and bibliographies
- To find out the historical development of a subject
- Shows relative use of subjects

## IMPACT FACTOR

Impact factor was devised by Eugene Garfield. The Impact factor (IF) of a journal is the yearly average number of citations that articles published in the last two years in a given journal received. IF determines the relative importance of a journal in its discipline. Journals with higher impact factors are often deemed to be more important, or carry more intrinsic prestige in their respective fields, than those with lower values.

**Calculation :** In any given year, the two-year journal impact factor is the ratio between the number of citations received in that year for publications in that journal that were published in the two preceding years and the total number of "citable items" published in that journal during the two preceding years.

$$IF_y = \frac{\text{Citations}_y}{\text{Publications}_{y-1} + \text{Publications}_{y-2}}$$

It is explained as Impact Factor of 2016 will be calculated by dividing the total citations received in 2016 by the publications of 2015 plus publications of 2014. Impact factor helps in comparing journals and the author impact factor helps to identify the prominence of the author in the specific field of study.

## EIGEN FACTOR

The Eigen factor is another PageRank-type measure of journal influence with rankings freely available online. The Eigen factor™ score of a journal is an estimate of the percentage of time that library users spend with that journal.

## H- INDEX

H index is an author level metric which measures the productivity and citation impact of a scientist or an author. H-index was invented by Jorge Hirsch in 2005. An author has h index 'h' if his Np- number of papers have cited h times. Eg. If an author has 15 h=index then his 15 papers will be cited 15 times or more.

Citation reports in Web of Science and citation tracker in Scopus calculate the h-index of a search result. Harzing's Publish or Perish program calculates the h-index based on Google Scholar entries. Various proposals to modify the h-index in order to emphasize different features have been made. Bornmann et al., recently proposed 3 additional metrics, h2lower, h2center, and h2upper to give a more accurate representation of the distribution shape. Scientists with high h2upper percentages are perfectionists, whereas scientists with high h2lower percentages are mass producers.

## i10-INDEX

i10-index is the number of publications with at least 10 citations. In July 2011, Google Scholar started a tool, which allows scholars to keep track of their own citations and also produces an h-index and an i10-index.

## MAJOR CITATION INDEXING SERVICES

**Web of Science**: Earlier known as Web of Knowledge is a leading citation database covering multiple subjects and peer reviewed literature. WoS includes Science Citation Index (SCI), Social Sciences Citation Index (SSCI), Arts and Humanities Citation Index, Index Chemicus, and Current Chemical Reactions, covering about 8,700 leading journals in science, technology, social sciences, arts, and humanities, ISI Proceedings, ISI Essential Science Indicators, Journal Citation Reports (two editions: Science and Social Sciences), in-cites, Science Watch, ISI Highly Cited.com, Index to Organism Names, and Biology Browser.

Use of ISI Web of Knowledge is licensed to institutions such as universities and the research departments of large corporations on subscription basis. Earlier it was owned by Thomnson Reuters and now the Clarivate Analytics owns Web of Science.

**Scopus :** Scopus is one of the largest abstracting and citation database published by Elsevier. Scopus covers the disciplines science, technology, medicine, social science, arts and humanities. Scopus is subscription based paid database. The author metrics can be known by searching his / her ORCID. Very good data analytics are provided for analysing author, article or author performance over years.

**Google Scholar :** It is freely available to search and cite articles. It's a google product designed as search engine. It enables keyword search and advance search options provides author search etc. Individual author sign up is possible and can track the citations for their articles. They can also know who has cited their article. Author citation metrics are calculated and updated regularly.

SCImago Journal Rank (SJR) indicator The SJR is an open access, free journal citation metric, based on citation information from Scopus. SJR indicator is a measure of scientific influence of scholarly journals that accounts for both the number of citations received by a journal and the importance or prestige of the journals where such citations come from. The SJR indicator provides an alternative to the Impact Factor (IF).

Citation indexes provide authoritative, timely and prospective as well as retrospective in-depth access to the literature. Citation indexes also provide various indicators to evaluate the author impact in a subject. Through citation analysis, citation index provides journal ranking by giving information about what articles, themes, and topics were being published, cited, or ignored. The journal impact factor and indexes helps the authors to select the journals on performance basis to publish their articles. Many papers are not getting citations as they are published in substandard journals or journals with lesser viewers. The metrics helps to analyse the productivity and designation of a journal or article or author.

## REFERENCES


Bornmann L, Mutz R D, and Daniel H D. (2010). The h index research output measurement: Two approaches to enhance its accuracy. Journal of Informetric, 4(14).

Hoseth, Amy. (2011). Google Scholar. The Charleston Advisor. Doi 12. 10.5260/chara.12.3.36.

https://www.wiley.com/network/journaleditors/editors/journal-and-article-metrics-an-overview-2

https://www.elsevier.com/editors/journal-and-article-metrics

https://scholar.google.co.in/intl/en/scholar/citations.html

https://clarivate.com/webofsciencegroup/essays/concept-citation-indexing/

# 6
# Open Access Publishing

## OPEN ACCESS MOVEMENT

In 2002, the Budapest Open Access Initiative put forth the benefits of free access to scholarly content. The Budapest Initiative stood, "to accelerate research, enrich education, share the learning of the rich with the poor and the poor with the rich, make this literature as useful as it can be, and lay the foundation for uniting humanity in a common intellectual conversation and quest for knowledge."

Open Access was defined in the Budapest Initiative literally as, "permitting any users to read, download, copy, distribute, print, search, or link to the full texts of these articles, crawl them for indexing, pass them as data to software, or use them for any other lawful purpose, without financial, legal, or technical barriers other than those inseparable from gaining access to the internet itself. The only constraint on reproduction and distribution, and the only role for copyright in this domain, should be to give authors control over the integrity of their work and the right to be properly acknowledged and cited."

After 15 months from forming the Budapest Open Access Initiative (BOAI), in April 2003, Howard Hughes Medical Institute called a meeting to discuss better access to scholarly literature. The open-access journal was defined in that meeting as "free, irrevocable, worldwide, perpetual right of access to, and a license to copy, use, distribute, transmit, and display the work publicly and to make and distribute derivative works, in any digital medium for any responsible purpose, subject to proper attribution of authorship" and from which every article is "deposited immediately upon initial publication in at least one online repository" This was named as Bethseda Statement and the Bethseda Statement established the term "open access" to represent the initiatives which stood for making scientific literature available to all for free.

## MILESTONES IN OPEN ACCESS

Open access was not started on a fine morning. It took time to convince the authors and publishers to make their publications open (Banks,2015). The history begins from the year 2002, the Budapest Open Access Initiative was taken. In 2003, the Bethesda statement was published and the first open-access journal PLOS Biology was published. The year 2008 witnessed the US Congress approved the policy for making open all the research papers brought out with the funding of the National Institute of Health. This was made available through PubMed Open. The report of the Scholarly Publishing Roundtable, US stated the importance of open access and respecting the interests of publishers as well. By then in the United Kingdom also the wave of open access has begun. The Finch Report of 2012, strictly stated to publish open all the research papers which are the outcome of projects funded by the government agencies. US Office of Science directed that all the federal agencies must ensure that the research outputs are available in the public domain. In 2014, KIN consultants launched the Open Access Network for cost-sharing and sustainable development. The mounting subscription cost of journals both online and print makes it impossible for libraries to subscribe to the resources and thus the research outputs are unable to reach the researchers. The journals are in the reachability of a few.

## MODELS OF OPEN ACCESS

Open access are of different models. They are –

- Golden Open access model
- Green Open access model
- Hybrid Open access model
- Bronze Open access model
- Diamond / Platinum Open access model, and
- Black Open access model

**Gold open access model :** An author publishes his/her article in an online open-access journal or book or any other source backed by an open-access publisher.

**Green open access model :** In Green open access an author publishes his article in any journal or book or other source and then self-archives it in open access institutional or other archives mostly a repository, or on a website after the embargo period if applicable. When compared, gold open access has the advantage of making publications freely accessible from the first day of its publication, which means the article or the content can be accessed immediately. Besides, the open-content licenses associated with, the gold open access provides wide exploitation rights, and immediate access and visibility so that the publication is widely used and cited by scholars.

Green open access does not provide the same legal content licensing and the usage is only permitted within the legal restrictions of copyright law. That means that the author's contract has to be carefully reviewed to enable an article to be re-used in a way that fulfills all the legal formalities. There is no specific rule governing the open accessibility of publications because different publishing houses have different embargo periods before making the articles freely available.

**Hybrid Open access model :** Hybrid open access journals contain a mixed type of articles like some are open and some are closed.

**Bronze Open access model :** Bronze open access journals provide the facility to read the article from the publisher's website and are not available for re-use.

**Diamond/ Platinum open access model :** Diamond/ Platinum open access allows authors to publish their articles without any charge or article processing fee.

**Black open access :** Black Open Access also exists like SciHub, where unauthorized digital copying is done.

## CREATIVE COMMONS LICENSES

Creative Commons (CC) is a non-profit organisation that releases pre-formulated copyright licenses which give creators great flexibility in communicating which rights they reserve and which rights they waive when it comes to other people using their work. By default, copyright law reserves all exploitation rights exclusively for the copyright holder and excludes anyone else from exploiting a copyrighted work, so the Creative Common system introduces a more flexible means by which authors can control how they wish to share their works.

Creative Commons licenses can only be granted to works that are subject to copyright and can only be granted by the holder of the exploitation rights. That means that CC licenses cannot be granted by authors who have signed over all their exploitation rights to a publisher or who have only retained non-exclusive usage right.

For research data CC licenses can only be granted if they have a certain originality and copyright is applicable. For instance, this does not apply to measurement data. In case of doubt case-by-case review is necessary. Creative Commons licenses are not recommended for software. The validity of a Creative Commons license is determined by the validity of the copyright.

Creative Commons licenses are a form of open content license. Other open content licenses include the General Public

License (GNU) for software licensing and various alternatives to CC licenses. However, CC licenses are probably the most widespread option. They are even used by scientific publishers who run open-access programs such as BioMed Central and SpringerOpen.

Creative Commons (CC) licences are composed of different elements or conditions. These conditions are combined to create a license that meets the creator's needs and grants the required exploitation rights. Each condition is represented by an acronym:

- Attribution: BY
- Non-commercial use: NC
- No derivative works: ND
- Share-alike: SA

Mixing and matching these elements produces a total of six commonly used licenses:

- CC-BY: Attribution
- CC-BY-ND: Attribution, no derivative works
- CC-BY-NC: Attribution, non-commercial use
- CC-BY-NC-ND: Attribution, non-commercial use, no derivative works
- CC-BY-NC-SA: Attribution, non-commercial use, share-alike
- CC-BY-SA: Attribution, share-like

The use of the relevant acronyms makes it immediately clear how the work may be used.

Since Creative Commons licenses are non-exclusive, additional individual agreements may be concluded with entities such as publishers to grant additional rights. Permission must be sought for any usage that goes beyond the conditions stipulated in the license. From the range of the licenses mentioned above, only CC-BY and CC-BY-SA are in accordance with the open access definitions. Although several usage rights are granted the author's personal/ moral rights are preserved.

## OPEN ACCESS PUBLISHERS

These are the organisations that promote OA publishing. A few Open Access publishing platforms are discussed here. SPARC (The Scholarly Publishing and Academic Resources Coalition) is a global coalition for open access, open data and open education. SPARC focuses on collaborating with other stakeholders – including authors, publishers, libraries, students, funders, policymakers and the public – to build on the opportunities created by the Internet, promoting changes to both infrastructure and culture needed to make open the default for research and education.

The key to SPARC's success is the commitment of its members to support and shape their initiatives. The members are primarily academic and research libraries located in the U.S. and Canada, who use the resources and support provided by SPARC to actively promote Open Access to scholarly articles, the open sharing of research data, and the creation and adoption of Open Educational Resources on their campuses.

Open Access Scholarly Publishing Association (OASPA) aims to bring together the scholarly community through leadership and development, collaboration and convening, setting standards, innovations and supporting open access ecosystem.

DOAJ or Directory of Open Access Journals is a resource where one can search and find a journal the article can be published with free access. Almost all the subject category are available from across the globe in DOAJ.

Springer Open Choice is another platform where an author can publish his work in public domain and ensure free access. Taylor and Francis Open is also providing opportunity to publish and access the resources freely.

PLoS - Public Library of Science is another journal where the works can be published as OA content. Wiley Open Access, Elsevier's Open Access Journals, Open Humanities Press, Media Commons Press, MLA Commons, etc. are examples. Open repositories or institutional repositories also acts as Open Access Publishing platforms.

As the open access publishing platforms offer free access to readers' they adopt many financial models to cover the cost of publishing. They often get back the cost incurred from subscriptions by institutions and individuals. Article processing charge may be recovered from authors. The beneficiaries of the OA publishing is the developing countries who cannot afford the rising price of scholarly content. Most of the publishers are from developed countries. Even the scholars in United States and United Kingdom and other developed countries raising their voice against the publishers who are charging high prices for articles. Many institutions are putting ban on subscription of such publishers. But the Open Access Movement is still in its infancy and the monopolists are gaining the business.

## REFERENCES

Banks, M. (2015). Open Access Publishing. *American Libraries, 46*(9/10), 58-61. Retrieved January 31, 2021, from http://www.jstor.org/stable/24604170

Berlin Declaration on Open Access to Knowledge in the Sciences and Humanities (2007), available at http://oa.mpg.de/openaccess-berlin/berlindeclaration.html

Budapest Open Access Initiative (2002), available at https://www.budapestopenaccessinitiative.org/read

https://openscience.com/green-oa-vs-gold-oa-which-one-to-choose/

https://www.publisso.de/en/advice/publishing-advice-faqs/creative-commons/

https://creativecommons.org/

https://openscience.com/green-oa-vs-gold-oa-which-one-to-choose/

Li Zhang, S. (2007). *The flavors of open access. OCLC Systems & Services: International Digital Library Perspectives, 23(3), 229–234.*

https://sparcopen.org/who-we-are/

# 7
# Information Laws

Information law is a broad term, which includes legal aspects of collection, organisation, storing, dissemination, access and use of information. Information can broadly be categorised in to three in the legal point of view. They are:-

I. Information governed by Government / Government agencies

II. Information created by Persons

III. Personal Information

There is no a single international law handling all these issues, while each country there are their own separate laws to handle the same. The following laws handle these issues. They are :-

1. Right to Information Acts / Freedom of Information - Information governed by government Acts.
2. Copyright laws- Information created by persons.
3. Personal information laws - Personal Information

These three categories of laws of India, USA and UK have been pointed out here.

## I - INFORMATION GOVERNED BY GOVERNMENT INDIA – RIGHT TO INFORMATION ACT, 2005

Right to Information Act was enacted in India in 2005. Before this act, there was an act named as in UK and USA, ie Freedom of Information Act which was passed in 2002. This law was replaced by the RTI Act of 2005. RTI Act 2005 covers all Indian states except Jammu & Kashmir state. Jammu & Kashmir has separate RTI Act which was enacted in 2009. As per this law any citizen of India has right to get the information which is kept by the government except information having confidentiality. As per the act the government offices are obliged to provide information needed by citizen. Here the query for the information is to be addressed to the Public Information Officer (POI) of concerned government office.

Fee of RTI request is Rs.10 which can be payable as DD (Demand draft) or IPO (Indian Postal Order) in favor of Public Information Officer of concerned office. The additional charge of photocopy / print is Rs 2 per page and Rs 50 per floppy / CD. As per this act, the citizen has special right to inspect the record he needed and the public authority shall charge no. fee for the first hour. But a fee of Rs. 5 for each subsequent hour shall be charged. Citizens belongs to below poverty line (BPL) category, he is not required to pay any fee.

The answer shall be given by the concerned authority to the seeker within 30 days of the receipt of the query. If an applicant is not receiving the information within the prescribed time or he is not satisfied with the information furnished to him, he can submit an appeal to the first appellate authority who is an officer senior in rank to the Public information Officer. Such an appeal, should be filed within a period of thirty days from the date on which the limit of 30 days.

Certainly there are few exceptions from disclosure of information. They are - Information which affect the sovereignty and integrity of nation, Information which results the contempt of court, Information which will cause breach of privilege of parliament, Information regarding trade secret or Intellectual property, Personal information, Information which would result threat of life of person of society.

## USA - Freedom of Information Act (FOAI)

Freedom of Information Act (FOAI) was passed in USA in 1966. This law allows citizens to know the information which is kept by Federal executive agencies of United states which include internal revenue service, defense departments etc.

FOIA insists three methods for the information disclosure. They are –

1. Publication in the Federal register, FOIA requires that agency regulations and procedural rules be automatically published in the Federal register.
2. Make available in the agency reading rooms. FOIA insists that certain other documents be made available for public access and copying in agency reading rooms unless they are available in other sources. These documents include (1) final opinions and orders in agency adjudications, (2) policy statements and interpretations adopted by an agency but not published in the Federal Register, (3) administrative staff manuals and instructions to staff that affect members of the public, and (4) copies of records that have previously been furnished in response to a FOIA request and which the agency has reason to believe are likely to be requested again in the future.
3. FOIA Requests - If information needed to one person is not available under the first two options, request can be given to the concerned authority for getting the same. Each Federal agency has its own wing to handle these queries. This service is free of cost, but reasonable amount will be levied in some cases as searching fee and dispatching fee. The law insists that, all queries are to be

answered within twenty working days. If the seeker is not satisfied with the answers, they can give appeal to the higher authority.

There are nine exemptions to the FIOA of United States as such laws in other nations. They are - Information regarding National security (This information is known as classified information pursuant to a presidential executive order), Internal agency rules (The information internal in nature of an agency or department is exempted from FOIA which is treated as predominately internal in nature and which do not possess any public interest), information exempted by another federal statute (there are some confidential information which are prohibited to get accessed by public. They are exempted here also), trade secrets (trade secrets and confidential commercial information are withhold by agencies for protecting financial exploitation), Information kept by Internal agencies. (These types of information include such as inter agency or intra agency communications such as letters memos etc.

## UK- Freedom of Information Act- UK

Freedom of information Act was passed in United Kingdom (FOIA-UK) in 2000. FOIA-UK covers in England, Wales and Ireland. A separate act was passed in Scotland in 2002, which is known as FOIA Scotland. The bud of this act was a white paper entitled "your right to know" published by the Government in 1997.

FOIA ensures the statutory right to access information related with public authorities, publicly owned companies and designated bodies performing public functions in UK. The act covers not only official documents but also information such as drafts, notes, e-mails, recorded telephones, CCTV recordings etc.

The request for information as per FOIA can be given by any person. It can be any citizen or a legal entity in UK and other countries and the motive behind the demand of information need not to specify. Information can be sought in any form ie either in printed of electronic form. Normally the service is free. But the department can charge the normal expenses such as postage, xerox charge, recording charge etc. The reply also can be in different means. The requester can opt the means of communication. Normally the answer is given within 20 working days and if it is needed more time it is to be intimated to the requester.

There are certain exceptions to FOIA- UK, they are - information which is available the to applicant by other means, information intended for future publication, information related with security matters of the country and National security, information related with defense, information related with international relations, information related with the economy of country, information resulted by Investigations and proceedings conducted by public authorities, information of law enforcement, court records, etc, information related with health and safety, environmental information, personal Information etc.

## II. INFORMATION CREATED BY PERSONS

Copyright laws are exclusive laws of governments to protect information created by persons. Copyrights are a set of exclusive rights granted by law to the creators or producers of forms of creative expressions such as literary, musical, artistic and cinematographic works. The rights are protections to the copyright owner. These rights provide the copyright owner the control over the use of his/ her works like their reproduction and distribution for a limited period of time. The creator of a work can prohibit or authorize its reproduction in various forms, including printing, recording, broadcasting, public performance translation or adaptation.

There are two theories behind copyright (Hombal,S.G and Prasad, K.N 2012), economic protection theory and moral argument theory. The economic protection theory says that, creativity in society is a good thing. In order to encourage creativity, the creator needs incentives. Such incentive includes providing limited monopolies with an economic value, such that the author can sell or dispose of his creation for monitory benefit. The moral rights theory argues that, there is an intangible relation between a creator and creation and this relationship remains even after the sale of creation.

There is an international law governing copyright. It is known as agreement of Berne Convention for the Protection of Literary and Artistic Works. According to this agreement works originating in one of the contracting country must be given the same protection in each of the other contracting countries as the latter grants to the works of its own nationals.

## India – Indian Copyright act, 1957

In India, copyright act was passed in 1914 (www.copyright.gov.in). It was an imitation of the British copyright act 1911, which was suitably modified in the context of British India. The present copyright act was passed in 1957. The Copyright Act, 1957 came into effect from January 1958. This Act has been amended six times since then, i.e., in 1983, 1984, 1992, 1994, 1999 and 2012. The Copyright (Amendment) Act, 2012 is the most significant one especially in this ICT era.

The statutory definition of copyright in India vide section 14 of the copyright act, 1957 is, "right to do or authorize others to do certain acts in respect of literary, dramatic or musical works, artistic work, cinematographic film, and sound recording". In short journal articles, books, computer programmes, songs, videos etc will come under this law. The owner ship of copyright is defined under Section 17 of the Act. In the case of a literary work (except computer programme), the copyright owner will get the exclusive rights to - reproduce the work, translate the work, issue copies of the work to the public, perform the work in public, communicate the work to the public and to make any adaptation of the work. In addition to all the rights applicable to literary works, owner of copyright of a computer programme will get the rights to sell or give on hire or offer for sale or hire, regardless of whether such a copy has been sold or given or hire on earlier occasion.

The duration of copyright lasts for 60 years. In the case of original literary, dramatic, musical and artistic works the 60-year period is counted from the year following the death of the author. In the case of cinematograph films, sound recordings, photographs, posthumous publications, anonymous and pseudonymous publications, works of government and works of international organisations, the 60-year period is counted from the date of publication.

Certain exceptions are there in the case of Indian copyright act. They are - use for personal, study, research, critical and review purpose. In this case reproduction is allowed and it will not be considered as copyright infringement. As per the section In section 52 clause (1)(O), it allowed taking maximum three copies of a document for public library. As per 52 clause (1) (n), libraries can digitize the work which they possess the hard copy. But it very clearly mentioned that the purpose is for preservation.

## United Kingdom – British Copyright Act, 1956

The United Kingdom is often considered to be the birthplace of the modern system of copyright law. In 16 century the printer organization (stationers Company) in Uk receive special right to printers (not to authors) exclusive rights to print and distribute books. After the Anglo-Scottish Union of 1707, the author gained the exclusive 'right and liberty' of printing books through the Statute of Anne 1709. As per this law the duration of right was confined to 14 years only. Later copyright law was passed in UK in 1956. The present copy right law in UK is Copyright, Designs and Patents Act 1988.

Copyright, Designs and Patents Act 1988 cover – literary (song lyrics, manuscripts, manuals, computer programs, commercial documents, leaflets, newsletters and articles etc.), dramatic (Plays, dance, etc.), musical, artistic (photography, painting, architecture, technical drawings/ diagrams, maps, logos, etc.), typographical arrangement of published editions (magazines, periodicals, etc.), sound recordings (musical and literary.) and films (broadcasts and cable programmes.).

Duration of each item under the act is as follows -

1. For literary, dramatic, musical or artistic works - 70 years from the end of the calendar year in which the last remaining author of the work dies, or the work is made available to the public, by authorised performance, broadcast, exhibition, etc.
2. Sound Recordings and broadcasts - 50 years from the end of the calendar year in which the last remaining author of the work dies, or the work is made available to the public, by authorised release, performance, broadcast, etc.
3. Films - 70 years from the end of the calendar year in which the last principal director, author or composer dies, or the work is made available to the public, by authorised performance, broadcast, exhibition, etc.
4. Typographical arrangement of published editions - 25 years from the end of the calendar year in which the work was first published.

Certain exceptions are there in this law. Fail dealing clause is there, for research and private study. The clause 29 says this. Section 29 of the Copyright Designs and Patents Act 1988 Act now reads as follows:

**29(1)** Fair dealing with a literary, dramatic, musical or artistic work for the purposes of research for a non-commercial purpose does not infringe any copyright in the work provided that it is accompanied by a sufficient acknowledgement (emphasis added).

**(1B)** No acknowledgement is required in connection with fair dealing for the purposes mentioned in subsection (1) where this would be impossible for reasons of practicality or otherwise.

**(1C)** Fair dealing with a literary, dramatic, musical or artistic work for the purposes of private study does not infringe any copyright in the work (emphasis added).

**(2)** Fair dealing with the typographical arrangement of a published edition for the purposes of research or private study does not infringe any copyright in the arrangement.

**(3)** Copying by a person other than the researcher or student himself is not fair dealing if –

**(b)** ... the person doing the copying knows or has reason to believe that it will result in copies of substantially the same material being provided to more than one person at substantially the same time and for substantially the same purpose.

## United States - US Copyright Law

Even though America was one of the colonies of Brittan, Statute of Anne of 1710 did not apply to the American colonies, Since it was an agrarian society. Before the commencement of a common Copyright law in 1790, there separate copyright laws in each states except Vermont. Copyright law of 1790 granted rights of printing, publishing and vending a work for 14 years, with an option of renewable term of additional 14 years. In 1831 US congress extended the initial term of fourteen years to 28, while the extension period continued as 14 fourteen years. In 1909 the renewal term was extended to 28 years. Thus period of protection became 56 years. In 1976, US Congress dramatically extended the period in 50 years after the death of author or 75 years after the date of publication in the case of works for hire. The present existing law of United States is Copyright Law of 1976.

In 1998, Congress passed the Digital Millennium Copyright Act (DMCA). The law became effective in October 2000 and it has been incorporated into the Copyright Act (Title 17 of the U. S. Code). This landmark legislation updated U.S. copyright law to meet the demands of the Digital Age and to conform U.S. law to the requirements of the World Intellectual Property Organization (WIPO) and treaties that the U.S. signed in 1996.

US Copyright Act also covers the following- literary works, musical works, including any accompanying words, dramatic works, including any accompanying music, pantomimes and choreographic works, pictorial, graphic, and sculptural works, motion pictures and other audiovisual works, sound recordings; and architectural works.

Duration of American Copyright act depends on the date of publication and whether it was published or not. Thus three different time limits are there.

(a) Created on or after January 1 1978.- This is governed by statutory section 17 USC

**302.** According to this section, a work that is created on or after January first, 1978 is given a term enduring for the author's life plus an addition of 70 years after author's death. In the case of joint work, It is last for 70 years after the death of last surviving author. In the case of work made for hire/ anonymous and pseudonymous works, duration of copyright is 95 years from the publication or 120 from the creation, whichever is shorter.

(b) Created before 1978, but not published. This is governed by statutory section 17 USC

**303.** According to this section, the duration of copyright of these works is same as works created after January 1, 1978.

(c) Created and published or registered before 1978. This is governed by statutory section 17 USC 304. According to this section, copyright duration is for a first term of 28 years from the date it was secured and during the last year of its first term a renewal for 28 year is possible.

Section 107 of the act gives provision of faire use for the academic community. As per this, "the fair use of a copyrighted work, including such use by reproduction in copies or phonorecords or by any other means specified by that section, for purposes such as criticism, comment, news reporting, teaching (including multiple copies for classroom use), scholarship, or research, is not an infringement of copyright". Section 108 provides libraries and archives certain relaxation. According this section, "it is not an infringement of copyright for a library or archives, or any of its employees acting within the scope of their employment, to reproduce no more than one copy or phonorecord of a work".

## III. PERSONAL INFORMATION LAW

Personal information law refers to the set of laws, policies and procedures, which aim to eliminate and minimise intrusion into one's privacy caused by the collection, storage and dissemination of personal data. Personal information is synonymously used as personally identifiable information, sensitive personal information, data protection and private information, which include any information that identifies a person, such as - personal identity details name, bio-metric information, contact information, financial information, Health information etc. There are different laws in different countries for the protection of this personal information, which are known in different names such as - data protection law, information privacy law, law of protection of personal information etc. Protection of personal information in India, USA and UK has been briefly pointed out here.

### India

Presently in India, there is no a concrete and specific law dealing with privacy and data protection. Presently cases regarding personal data are handled by Section 420 in the

Indian Penal Code (Cheating and dishonestly inducing delivery of property), Section 420 in the Indian Penal Code (Dishonest Misappropriation of property) and certain sections in the IT act, 2000 of India, viz sec 43(a) which deals with unauthorised access of information and sec 72(a), which deals with disclosure of confidential information.

Recently, a private bill was tabled in the Lok Sabha, by a Member of Parliament Baijayant "Jay" Panda. It is known as Data (Privacy and Protection) Bill, 2017, proposing the right to privacy as a fundamental right for Indian citizens.

**US**

Presently there is no single and comprehensive national (federal) law dealing with collection and use of personal information, however there are several state laws governing personal information. In addition to these laws there are some "best practices", they are guidelines, developed by different government agencies and industry groups that do not have the force of law, but are part of self-regulatory guidelines and frameworks.

The important federal (national) containing the parts of information laws are -

The Federal Trade Commission Act / FTCA (15 U.S.C. §§41-58) - This Federal law was established in 1914. The motives of this act were to create Federal Trade Commission (FTC) and to give US government a complement of legal tool in the case of business for fair competition in business and protection of consumers from fraudulent business practices.

The Health Insurance Portability and Accountability Act of 1996(HIPAA). This act was passed in 1996. This law requires the protection and confidential handling of protected health related information of citizens.

Family Educational Rights and Privacy Act (FERPA). This was enacted in 1974.This law provides parents certain protections with regard to their children's education records, such as report cards, transcripts, disciplinary records, contact and family information, and class schedules.

The Children's Online Privacy Protection Act (COPPA). This is a U.S. federal law designed to limit the collection and use of personal information about children by the operators of Internet services and Web sites, which was Passed by the U.S. Congress in 1998, the law took effect in April 2000.COPPA is the first U.S. privacy law written for the Internet.

In addition to these federal laws, there are some state laws in United states. The prominent among them are - California Online Privacy Protection Act, California Financial Information Privacy Act, California Shine the Light Law, Information Security Breach and Notification Act of New York, Social Security Number Protection Law of New York etc.

**UK**

Data Protection Act (DPA) of UK was passed in 1998 in UK. Recently UK passed Data protection Act 2018 and thus the act of 1998 was superseded and the latest one is capable to handle personal information in the digital age. It is a national law which complements the

European Union's General Data Protection Regulation (GDPR). DPA covers personal information including processed information in both automated & printed forms and personal information possessed by Government.

The law protect the sensitive personal information such as – race, ethnic background, political opinions, religious beliefs, trade union membership, genetics, biometrics (where used for identification), health, sex life or orientation. As per this act, there are certain rights given to each citizen, they are – right to be informed about how personal data is being used, right to access personal data, right to correct incorrect data, stop or restrict the processing of data in certain circumstances.

## REFERENCES


Copyright Office. (n.d.). Retrieved August 01, 2018, from *http://copyright.gov.in/*

E. (2018, January 12). Digital Millennium Copyright Act. Retrieved July 14, 2018, from http://www.ala.org/advocacy/copyright/dmca

F. (2009, November 25). Intellectual property issues within India working with the authorities. Retrieved August 14, 2018, from *https://de.slideshare.net/tony. ridley/intellectual-property- issues-within-india-working-with-the-authorities.*

History of the DMCA. (2010, December 01). Retrieved August 27, 2018, from https://bcgrouptwo.wordpress.com/about/

Main Page. (August). Retrieved August 18, 2018, from *https://en.wikipedia.org/wiki/Main_Page.*

Office, U. C. (n.d.). Chapter 11: Subject Matter and Scope of Copyright. Retrieved August 30, 2018, from https://www.copyright.gov/title17/92chap1.html

Participation, E. (n.d.). Freedom of Information Act 2000. Retrieved June 23, 2018, from *http://www.legislation.gov.uk/ukpga/2000/36/contents.*

Service, U. C. (n.d.). UK copyright law. Retrieved August 30, 2018, from https://www.copyrightservice.co.uk/copyright/p01_uk_copyright_law.

Service, U. C. (n.d.). UK copyright law: A summary. Retrieved July 01, 2018, from https://www.copyrightservice.co.uk/copyright/uk_law_summary.